WHEN I GROW UP,
I WANT TO BE A WRITER

by

Cynthia MacGregor

Contents:

Part Two: Other Kinds of Writing to Try

Slogans

Creative Menus

Reviews

Limericks

Advertisements

Lyrics

Family or Neighborhood Newsletter

Word Puzzles and Games

Greetings!

Aesop Revisited

Balloons That Don't Float

Speeches

Diaries and Journals

Funny, But Not on Your Report Card

Captions Outrageous

Part Three: The End of This Book Is Just the Beginning

FOREWORD: THIS BOOK GIVES HOMEWORK!

This book had its origin in a class I taught some time ago. When my daughter started junior high, she found out that in that school Tuesday afternoons were unique. Instead of regular classes, the kids had a variety of special classes to choose from. Many of these were taught by parents with particular skills.

When the program was announced, my daughter immediately volunteered me. "My mom's a writer!" Laurel offered. "She could teach creative writing." I quickly found myself in the principal's office. I wasn't being told to stay after school! But I was being asked to come in and teach every Tuesday.

The kids were free to choose from among the various Tuesday afternoon classes. I was pleased at how many kids signed up for creative writing. Then I gave the Dreaded Announcement: "You can't learn writing just by hearing me talk about it. You have to actually write. But if you spend all your class time writing, you won't have a chance to learn anything from me. So I'll be teaching you in class, then giving you writing assignments for homework."

You can imagine the reaction that announcement got! I heard groans. I heard protests. "But none of the other Tuesday afternoon classes gives homework."

"Sorry, kids," I told them, "but I've already cleared it with the principal. You lose. Now, you know attendance in this class is voluntary. If you don't want homework, you can transfer into one of the other classes. If you want to learn creative writing, you're stuck doing homework."

A few kids did transfer out. But in the next few weeks, I had more than that number transfer into the class. They wanted to learn creative writing. They'd heard it was a good class. And they were willing to do homework.

4

You have to be willing, too. This isn't a book you just sit and read. No one ever learned to be a better writer merely by reading someone's instructions. You have to practice writing. You have to sharpen your skills. You have to refine your craft.

But if you own this book, either you or a relative or friend bought it knowing you have an interest in writing. And if you're interested in writing, then doing a little writing shouldn't really feel like homework. It should be something you enjoy doing very much.

If you don't do the exercises, the writing practice I've assigned throughout the book, you're not going to get much out of the book. If you're not willing to practice, exchange this book for another one. Buy something you can read just for fun, a book that makes no demands of you.

This book gives homework.

INTRODUCTION

What makes a good writer?

There are probably almost as many answers to that question as there are people who want to be writers. Let's start with one very important answer, though: A good writer writes work that other people enjoy reading. Whether it's fiction or nonfiction, it grabs the reader's interest. If it's fiction, it's believable (even if it's set in a far-off galaxy). The words sparkle like polished rubies. The descriptions spark vivid pictures in the reader's mind. The writing flows.

The purpose of this book is to help you be a better writer. I'm assuming you're taking English classes in school. I'm assuming you know much of the basics—that "but" is a conjunction, and "write" is a verb, and "I ain't got none of them new books yet" is a sentence that's in a lot of trouble. As is the person who said it.

I'm assuming you're learning, in school, most of the rules of proper English grammar and usage. That's not what this book is about. (In fact, you may have noticed that I broke one of those rules in the paragraph above—I used a sentence fragment. Once you've learned the rules, you can start learning which ones you may break, and when.)

This book will give you a chance to play around with a few different kinds of writing you may not have tried in school. More than that, it will show you some ways to improve your skills—your craft—as a writer.

I hope you enjoy it. I hope you learn a lot from it. Go through this book as slowly or as quickly as you want. When you've finished reading it and doing all the exercises in it, it might be helpful to go through the book again. This time, when you work on the earlier exercises, you'll have the knowledge you gained from the later ones.

And what if you're not sure of your career plans— what if you aren't sure you want a career as a writer? This book is really for all kids who enjoy writing, whether or not they plan to be novelists, journalists, poets, or playwrights, ad copywriters, or any other kind of professional writers. Good writing is important in many careers, not only for authors.

For instance, businesspeople often need to write crisp, clear reports, persuasive sales letters, and other forms of communications. People working in publicity and public relations, personnel managers who have to write employee handbooks, and those who work in many other fields as well need to write well. Or you may find yourself in a career in which you're called on to give speeches— which you first need to write.

Good writing is important in everyday life, too. If you needed to write to your local Consumer Affairs Department, explaining persuasively how you were treated unfairly by a local store, would you be able to write an effective, easily understood letter?

And if you plan to be a writer, but not to write stories or articles, books or plays or poems, you still need to communicate well. Cookbook writers aren't concerned with plot and dialogue, but they still need to write clear, easy-to-follow instructions.

This book is divided into three parts. Part One deals with some of the basics you need to learn and practice in order to improve your writing. You'll learn about writing good dialogue, dreaming up titles, making your characters seem more believable, and lots more.

These skills will help you no matter what field of writing you want to get into. So please don't skip the dialogue lessons just because your interest is in poetry, or skip the poetry lessons just because your interest is in news reporting.

Besides, life is funny. You may think you know where your career is headed, or what your interests are, but life often hands us surprises. When I was your age (don't you hate that expression?), I never imagined I'd one day write a book for kids on how to be a better writer. The more you learn about all the different aspects of writing, the better your writing will get, regardless of what kind of writing you do.

This book doesn't pretend to tell you everything that you need to know in order to be a good writer. But, added to the basics you're learning in your English classes, this book will give you a good head start in your career—or hobby—of writing. For one thing, since the book covers many kinds of writing, it doesn't explore any of them in great depth. Whole books have been written on plotting fiction, writing dialogue, or crafting poetry.

Part Two of the book offers suggestions for different kinds of writing projects you can try your hand at now, other than the usual stories, essays, and articles. They'll give you good experience and good practice, and they may make you aware of types of writing you never thought of. They may even point you down a different career path within the field of writing than whatever you may have in mind now. Again, it's good to try all the different projects, even those that are far off from where you think your future career lies.

Finally, Part Three asks you to try some more traditional forms of writing, using the skills you've learned in this book.

So now you know what this book is about. Ready? Get set. Write on!

PART ONE:

Some of the Basics

WHATYAMACALLIT

"Sticks and stones may break my bones, but names can never harm me." True or false? False, if the "name" in question is the title of your story, article, book, or other writing. The titles you give your writing can do you a great deal of good—or harm.

You need to arouse the reader's interest—and, even before that, you need to get the editor's attention. If you don't, your work may get skipped over. The editor whose interest isn't grabbed by your title may shuffle your manuscript to the bottom of the pile. If it does eventually get published, the newspaper or magazine reader who's not intrigued by your title may jump to another story or article.

If your work is a book, your title is even more important. With a published article, story, essay, or poem, the reader is already reading the magazine, newspaper, or anthology. It's harder for him to ignore your work even if the title doesn't reel him in. A potential book reader, though, can more easily bypass the whole thing. Thousands of books stand next to each other on the shelves of the bookstore or library. You need a title that will reach out from the shelf and grasp a browsing reader by the collar.

A good title can either succinctly convey the topic of the book, story, or article or be deliberately obscure to arouse curiosity. Either way, it should tickle the reader's interest. It should make her want to open the book or turn to the story to see if it looks good. (After that, your writing needs to "sell" her on buying the book or continuing to read the story.)

Whether your title spells out the point of your book/article/story or deliberately leaves the reader wondering, "What's that about?" your title needs to get the reader's attention and to do it in very little space.

How do you dream up a suitable title?

• Once in a blue moon, the title is the first thing that suggests itself to you. You're not even trying to think of one, but it springs into your head. "Gee—what a great title!" you think—and now you need to write a book, article, or whatever to go with it.

• More frequently, you first decide to write on a particular subject. Keeping in mind both your general topic (for example, discipline problems in school) and the angle from which you're approaching it (for example, what effect they have on the other kids in school), you think of a suitable title. After that, you start writing the actual piece. (This is more true of nonfiction than of fiction.)

• Sometimes you know your topic but can't think of a good title no matter how hard you think. The title finally comes to you as you look through the finished piece. Perhaps it's a quotation from one of your fictional characters, or from the real person you are writing a profile of: "Liars Like Me," "The Only Orphan at the Picnic," and "Catastrophe Central" are examples of good potential titles that might be drawn from actual dialogue. Perhaps your title's source will be a bit of description from within the piece you've written. Here are some provocative titles that might have come from description within a piece: "The Bare, Grey Room," "A Carload of Clowns," "Not a Laughing Matter."

Your first homework assignment is a three-parter. For the first part, think of ten existing titles that have intrigued you. They can be titles of books, stories, articles, or essays, even poems or plays. The important thing is that the title reached out and grabbed you.

Now stop and analyze what it was about these titles that got your attention. Did a title make a specific promise or challenge that appealed to you, like "How To Be More Popular in Ten Steps" or "Finish Your Homework Faster"? Did a title intrigue you because you didn't know what it referred to, like "Violent Violets"? Did a title pique your interest and make you want to learn more, like "Too Big a Secret"?

Your next assignment is to write ten good, grabby titles of your own. They may be suitable for any kind of writing, any length. The only requirement is that they should be designed to get a reader's attention. They should make a potential reader interested in reading the actual article, story, book, or whatever.

For the last part of your first homework, I'll supply brief descriptions of some possible stories, articles, or books. Your challenge is to think of at least one suitable title for each:

• A boy finds out he was adopted and has to decide whether or not he wants to meet his birth parents.
• A girl owns a horse. The family's finances take a turn for the worse, and they have to sell the horse.
• A book for little kids about a child's first day in school.
• A comprehensive history of aviation.
• A serious nonfiction book for teenagers on a subject

they'd usually find boring. Think of a title that might intrigue them enough to pick up the book, yet is still appropriate to the subject matter and the serious tone of the book.

• A romance novel set in the Revolutionary period.
• Science fiction set in the year 2087 on this planet, involving androids and people living in undersea colonies.

IT WAS A DARK AND STORMY STORY

"Hi. I'm Cynthia."

That's a good way to start a conversation. But how do you start a story or an article?

Of course, if you're writing fairy tales, you can always start with "Once upon a time." But I'd be willing to bet not too many of you are planning to write fairy tales. And for a story about two best friends who have a misunderstanding, or a report on pollution in urban areas, or an essay on things parents say that make their kids tune out instead of listening, "Once upon a time" is not a very useful beginning!

No matter what you're writing, you need a great opening, or "lead," as it's sometimes called. (That's "lead" as in "You lead and I'll follow," not "lead" as in "You're dragging your foot like it's made of lead.")

The opening line "It was a dark and stormy night" is so much a cliché that it's become a joke. Yet at one time writers—too many writers—actually did begin their books or stories with that sentence. Another overused opening is any variation of the following sentence: "When John got out of bed that morning, he had no idea that his life would be completely changed by bedtime."

You can do better.

How are you going to begin your story or article? For nonfiction, often the best opening is a startling, interesting, or in some other way attention-grabbing fact: "Over twice as many robberies were reported to the Midville Police Department last year than the year before."

Another good opening is a question: "Are you one of the people who has heard the strange, unexplainable noises at night near the construction site on the corner of Franklin and Elm?"

The traditional way to begin a newspaper article is with the "five Ws": Who, What, When, Where, Why. "Mayor Thompson announced Monday, in a speech at City Hall, that because of widespread accusations of fraud in the recent election, a new election will be held next month." It's not imaginative or distinctive, but it does get the most information across in the least space.

Today, though, there is a growing trend for even some newspaper stories to have more creative openings. The old-fashioned "five Ws" opening is what's known as a straight reportorial approach. The writer is simply reporting facts.

For instance, using the straight reportorial approach, an article on poverty might begin:

Local charities last year helped 10,467 needy families or individuals, a 30 percent increase over last year. But many financially troubled people still aren't getting the help they need so badly.

Instead, some writers today might begin an article on the same topic this way:

Pacing the worn wooden floor of her sparsely furnished apartment, Joan tries not to dwell on the fact that there's no food in the house. But though Joan can ignore her own rumbling stomach, how will she explain the situation to her children? Angie, age two, and Todd, five, are too young to understand. They only stop crying for food long enough to ask where their daddy has gone.

In school, when your teachers assign essays or other writing, they probably give you a minimum number of pages, or words, to write. But when you write for a magazine or newspaper, you have to be concerned with a maximum as well. You may be told to keep your work to 3000 words, or to 750.

If you have limited space and have to cram a lot of facts into a small number of words, the straight reportorial lead is probably best. But painting a word picture of hungry Joan and her awful situation is going to get the attention of a lot more readers. People might skip reading an article that begins with some dry facts. Many of those same people, though, will read an article that starts out by telling about a person. Good description ("worn wooden floor," "sparsely furnished apartment") helps too.

Of course, the subject of your article, and your opening, doesn't have to be a person. Suppose you're writing an article on the importance of having cats and dogs neutered. Which of the following two openings is more likely to make you want to keep reading?

Officials at the local animal shelter performed 1,206 operations to neuter cats and dogs in the last year. During that time, they estimate the population of cats and dogs in our county grew by three times that number. Or:

Anita hates going to work on Thursdays. On Mondays, Tuesdays, Wednesdays, and Fridays, she gets up eager to go to work at the County Animal Shelter. Anita loves animals and loves working with them. But Thursday is the day that the shelter deals with its overpopulation problems. On that day, all animals that have been at the shelter for over two weeks are euthanized (killed in a merciful manner). Anita wishes she could call in sick every Thursday.

When you're writing fiction, it's tempting to start with a description:

The rustling leaves along the moonlit street sounded as if they were whispering. As the silvery moonbeams filtered through the shifting leaves, they

14

shone on Jeff and Judy, who were talking so intently that they didn't even notice the pungent scent of honeysuckle that the night breeze carried up and down the street.

It's tempting, but try to avoid that temptation, or at least keep the description short. It's better to start with something happening. Start with action:

"Fire!" the young boy screeched as he ran from the house, a plume of smoke following him out the door.
Or:

Kayla eluded her mother's grasp and darted across the busy street. Ignoring the oncoming traffic, she somehow managed to reach the far curb in one piece. Her mother, watching the cars speed by and hearing more than one car squeal to an abrupt stop, felt too jelly-legged to cross the street and catch up with Kayla.

Have something happen right at—or at least right near—the beginning of your story or book. Even if your first sentence is description, follow it quickly with action, or grab the reader's interest in some other way, such as by giving her something to wonder about. Let's play with the first sentence of that descriptive paragraph:

The rustling leaves along the moonlit street sounded like they were whispering. Catherine had the irrational fear that somehow they were repeating the awful secret she'd whispered in Anne's ear that morning.
Or:

The rustling leaves along the moonlit street sounded like they were whispering. Jim found himself actually standing there, listening, as if he could find an answer to his problem by listening to the trees "talk."
Or:

The rustling leaves along the moonlit street sounded like they were whispering. Marty, hidden on a high branch of one of the trees, strained to see if he could hear his mother's voice calling him. The leaves were the only sound, though. "I'll bet she doesn't even realize I'm missing," he thought.

Remember, there are lots of interesting books in the library or bookstore...lots of interesting stories or articles in any magazine...and lots of other activities besides reading that reach out for a person's attention. If a reader isn't hooked on your opening paragraph, he's likely to put down the magazine, or at least skip to the next story or article. Like a fisherman choosing the brightest lure or the plumpest worm, you've got to make the lead to your story, article, or essay, or the opening of your book the most attractive temptation you can find. Otherwise you won't reel a fish in.

Now write five good fiction leads and five good nonfiction leads.

IS THAT ALL THERE IS?

How are you going to end your story, essay, book, or article? You want the ending to be powerful, to pack a punch. When it's appropriate, you want your ending to be, in the words of the show-business newspaper Variety, "socko." (No, Socko isn't Nancy's comic strip friend—that's Sluggo!) Your ending should make an impact on the reader, whether you're writing fiction or nonfiction.

When ending fiction, make sure to wrap up all your loose ends, then find a good way to close the book or story, and make a graceful exit. Quickly. The climax of the book or story should be followed very shortly by the ending. Don't be like Beethoven and many other classical composers, who wrote symphonies with endings that dragged on and on. Just when it sounds like the symphony is over, the musicians start playing again.

Have you resolved all the questions the story or book raised? Do we know who stole Rob's bike, or what's making those ghostly looking lights in the windows of the deserted house? Has Josh been rescued from the wilderness? Did Margo succeed in getting Aaron's interest—or give up and decide to look for a boyfriend elsewhere? Great! Now wind the action down quickly, get your characters offstage, and lower the curtain. The story is over. Wrap it up in a sentence or a paragraph (or perhaps a few paragraphs, in the case of a book). Don't let it drag on.

With nonfiction, there are many types of closings that work. One of the most successful is to repeat the theme of your opening sentence or paragraph. Let's suppose you're writing about kids and drugs. Let's also suppose your lead is:

Kids make many mistakes, like ordering the "Wednesday Special Casserole" in Eisenhower Junior High School's cafeteria, or thinking they can study for a test at the last minute, on the schoolbus. But one of the biggest mistakes a kid can make is deciding to try drugs.

Repeating the opening theme in your closing, you might come up with a paragraph like this:

Kids make many mistakes. You can't learn your way around the world without a certain amount of trial-and-error. But if you know the consequences of doing drugs, there's one very serious mistake you can spare yourself the agony of making.

Sometimes presenting a powerful fact works well as a closing:

Maybe the best indicator of today's morality is this: An informal survey of 100 students at Middletown High revealed the fact that 68 percent admitted to having cheated on a test at least once. Perhaps the worst part is, most of the students showed no embarrassment, shame, or regret at this admission.

Another strong way to close an article or essay is to present the reader with a question or a challenge:

Now you know that the homeless man on the corner may not be a "lazy bum" who doesn't want to work. He may be a victim of hard times. He may have once had a job, a family, and a nice house—perhaps as recently as last year. Now, the dinner he gets at the soup kitchen may be the only thing he eats all day. The next time a raggedy, unshaven person approaches you for money on the street, how will you react?

Whether you're writing fiction or nonfiction, avoid overworked closings. One of the worst of these is "...but that's another story," as in, "I could tell you what Jim and Jerry did when they finally got the clubhouse built; but that's another story." (A good rule of thumb is: If it's a familiar-sounding closing, it's probably been overdone and should be avoided.)

You haven't done a good job of ending your story, essay, or article if you leave your readers thinking any of these things:
• Is that the end? Or is there more?
• But what happened to Jeff's grandmother?
• Isn't the writer ever going to finish wrapping up this story?
• I've heard this ending before!

WHO'S THERE?

In life, you recognize who's speaking not only by their voice but also by their speech habits. It could be a word they often use, the fact that they usually speak in long sentences—or short, choppy ones—the way they pepper their speech with slang, the fact that they speak in a formal manner, or some other habit or manner of speaking.

Listen to real people speaking. The school principal doesn't speak like your English teacher, who in turn doesn't sound at all like your mom. Your dad's voice is almost certainly lower than your mom's, but I am sure those are not the only differences in their speech.

Your best friend would never be mistaken for your aunt. Again, it's not just the audible voice that's different. If you saw, written on paper, a few sentences they'd spoken, you'd still know which of them was talking. Listen to people speaking. Try to catch the differences in how they speak. Does someone say "Right?" at the end of many sentences? Does another say "uh" between a lot of words? Does one of your friends often sound hesitant and unsure of himself? Does another always sound excited? Or emphatic? Does someone use a lot of long, less-common words? Make notes on each person's speech mannerisms. Analyze why these people sound different from each other.

Your fictional characters, too, should sound different from each other. When you're writing dialogue, it's easy to write it the way you yourself talk. It sounds natural to your ears, and you feel pleased with the real-sounding dialogue you've written.

But if your characters all sound like you, they also all sound like each other. And now you're facing two problems.

One problem is that not everyone talks like you do. If one of your characters is a dynamic executive, the head of a large corporation, do you think he or she is going to speak the way you do? Even if your characters are all kids, they won't speak identically to you and to each other. Do your friends all sound like you? Don't they have speech patterns that make their speech distinctive?

And that's the other problem. Not only do all your characters sound like you—when that's highly unlikely in real life—but they also all sound like each other.

Now, I'm not suggesting that every character has to have a distinctive voice. If you write a story in which you have ten characters, it's a bit much to try to give each a recognizably different speech pattern. It's all right if some of them sound pretty much like each other, especially if they're minor characters—people who don't play a big part in the book. It's all right if some of them sound like you, especially if they're around your age. But not all of them should sound like each other or like you. Not even most of them should.

Even if all the characters in your story are kids, it's highly unlikely their speech would be interchangeable. Try to at least give your most important characters distinctive speech patterns. And make sure your other characters sound believable for who they are. Most truck drivers don't sound like politicians. Most dads don't sound like their daughters.

In case you haven't learned this yet in school, here are some rules of the road:

• When you have a long passage of dialogue, and you start a new paragraph with the same person speaking, do not use close-quotation marks at the end of the first paragraph, but do use open-quotation marks at the start of the next paragraph.

• A period or a comma at the end of a quotation always goes inside the close-quotes. Place an exclamation point or question mark according to the sense of the sentence, however:

I asked, "Did you see him?" (The question is the quoted matter, so the question mark goes inside the close-quotes.)

Was it you who said "Hello"? (The entire sentence is the question, rather than the quoted matter being the question, so the question mark goes outsiide the close-quotes.)

Assignment: Write a page consisting mostly of dialogue in which two people with recognizably different speech patterns talk to each other. After each person has spoken one sentence, the reader should be able to tell which person is speaking even without "Jane said" and "John said."

Now here's some more homework: Think of four characters. Give each one a name. Try to make them different types, not four students, four housewives, four farmers, or four retired people. Now write down a few facts about each of these people you've just invented. You might include each one's age, personality, occupation ("student" or "retired" is acceptable here), and hobbies. Add anything else relevant to the characters that will help you get a better feel for who they are.

Now write a conversation among those four people, making sure each quotation sounds as if it really could have been spoken by that person.

I am not asking for a story here. No plot is needed. Just a conversation.

SHOW AND TELL

In elementary school, you're encouraged to "show and tell," but in writing you need to show more than you tell. Which of the paragraphs below is more descriptive and more interesting?

Mikey was in a very angry mood. His brother had never seen him like that before.

Or:

The first thing Howie noticed, when his brother Mikey walked in, was his scowl. It was so deep-set that Howie thought the frown lines might become permanently embedded in Mikey's face. Then Mikey slammed his books down on the desk. They bounced right off again, thudding onto the floor. Mikey actually growled as he bent to pick them up. Gathering his homework together, Howie left the room. It would be useless to try to study with the "bad mood rays" radiating out from Mikey like that.

The first paragraph tells you that Mikey is in a bad mood. You get the general idea, but you don't form much of a mental picture. The information isn't going to remain with you as strongly. The second paragraph shows you that Mikey is in a bad mood. The words "bad mood" don't

21

actually appear till the last sentence, but any reader will understand exactly what kind of mood Mikey is in long before reaching that sentence.

On the other hand, it takes a much longer paragraph to show Mikey's bad mood than to tell about it in two sentences. If you show all the information you want your readers to have, you'll wind up with a book about the size of the Encyclopedia Britannica! You need to use judgment in deciding what to tell and what to show.

There's no simple rule that governs all circumstances. Here are a few guidelines, though:

• Show more in a book; you have more space to play with. Tell more in a story; you have to keep it condensed.

• If it's background and it's not important, tell it and keep it brief. If it's important, or it sets the stage for what's going to happen next, or it's a detail you want made clear to your readers, or it helps define or delineate a character, show it.

• Showing some background details gives flavor to your story, but don't go overboard. For instance, suppose you are writing an article—or a story—about a woman who lives in a very modern building but has an apartment filled with antiques. You could simply say, "Despite the modern appearance of her glass-fronted high-rise, Julianne's apartment is filled with antiques." You've conveyed the essential information. But you've merely told. You haven't shown.

Now try a different approach:

The building is modern in appearance, from its big glass windows to its sky-grabbing height. But step inside Julianne's seventeenth-floor apartment and you may need a minute to adjust to the change in era. From the footworn antique throw rugs to the hand-crafted rocking chair, from the old-fashioned knicknacks perched on every surface to the stuffed owl on the coffee table, everything seems is if it might have come from your great-great-grandma's house.

Your reader has a much better feel for the study in contrast now, as well as knowing more specifically what Julianne's apartment is filled with. You could go on, giving still more details of the apartment, listing more of the items that line the shelves, describing the old-fashioned sofa or the quaint old phone. But chances are it would be overkill. Give the reader too much information and he'll tune out.

You can always insert some more description later in the article:

Julianne's modern clothing seemed somehow out of place as she settled back luxuriously into the cushions of the emerald green brocade sofa. In that room, she would have looked more appropriately attired in a dress with a bustle.

When I first wrote the paragraph above, I wrote "...she would have looked more appropriately attired in clothing from the 1800s." I replaced that with the sentence as you see it printed. "Clothing from the 1800s" tells. "A dress with a bustle" shows.

Certain kinds of writing demand more detail than others. In a romance novel, lush descriptions are more common than in many other kinds of novels. And mystery novels or stories sometimes require specific details that will later prove important to the action. If the reader is going to need to know, later on, that there's a secret panel in the wall, you'd better tell her up front that the wall is paneled. You probably don't want her to guess right away that there's going to be a secret panel, though. If that's the case, you'd better give other details about the room, letting the paneling be just one of many details you depict.

You can use dialogue as a means of showing instead of telling. Which of the following two paragraphs makes a stronger impression and paints a more vivid picture?

Angry at finding his science experiment ruined, Mikey demanded to know who had poured soap into the bottle. He exploded at his youngest brother, Howie, whom he suspected of having commited the "crime," and threatened to get back at him for it. It was a threat Howie fearfully believed.

Or:

Mikey screamed, "Who's the idiot who poured soap into this bottle? That's my science experiment! I need it for class tomorrow, and now some stupid moron has just— Howie, I'll clobber you! It was you, wasn't it?" His eyes bulged, and his face resembled the color of a sunset sky as he eyed his youngest brother suspiciously. "I'm gonna get you for this, man!" he seethed, his fierce scowl making Howie believe this was no empty threat.

Of course, there's more "showing" in that paragraph than just what's contained in the dialogue. But Howie's angry words go far toward conveying his mood.

Assignment: Rewrite each of the two paragraphs below, using description and, where it's suitable, dialogue.

First:

It was raining, and Liz had nothing to do. Talking to herself, she debated the possible activities she might find to take up her time on this dull, boring Saturday. She was gazing into the mirror, doing her best imitation of the principal, Ms. Wilson, when her pesty brother, Barry, walked into the room and immediately began living up to his reputation.

Second:

The run-down house had a reputation. Half the kids in the neighborhood believed at least one ghost lived there, if not a collection of them. And even the kids who refused to believe in ghosts refused just as insistently to walk past the house at night. They'd cross the street to avoid getting too close.

THE FIVE SENSES ARE WORTH MORE THAN A NICKEL

In both fiction and nonfiction, descriptions are important. Your readers want to see, hear, feel, and even smell and taste the surroundings you're writing about. They certainly want to know some physical description of the people, too. How much description depends on what you're writing about, and what genre (such as romance, mystery, or science fiction) you're writing in.

Certainly romance novels demand much more extensive description than children's books or nonfiction. A newspaper account of an auto accident calls for some physical description. A report on a political campaign probably doesn't need as much description, but some is still needed. Was the crowd at the rally restless? Attentive? Enthusiastic? Obstreperous?

Describing how something looks comes fairly naturally to most people. A dog might be large, shaggy, and brown. Moving beyond basic description, its coat might be matted, and its tail might droop like a flag on a windless day. On beyond even that, did it trot into the room eagerly, lie on the floor lazily, or stretch out contentedly?

But why stop there? Move beyond how it looked. How did it sound? Did the dog pant like an overweight man who's just tried to chase the mail truck for a block? Did he growl like a motor that's just starting up?

Feeling is yet another sense, and it may be applicable here too. If one of your characters pets the dog, did its fur feel in any way noteworthy? Was it silky, ruffled, smooth, abrasive, gritty, tangled, or shedding?

Smell is relevant too. Did the dog smell of skunk? Of its owner's perfume? Wet? Fresh and clean?

Though taste isn't applicable in this case, it will

be if you're describing a dinner, the ice cream cone your character is eating, or even the mud that gets into your hero's mouth when the bully pushes him down into the wet dirt.

You certainly can't describe every object in terms of all five senses; you don't even want to describe most objects you write about at all. Your book, story, or article would get so bogged down in description that your readers would give up and stop reading. But appropriate use of description, where it contributes something to the story, is a valuable part of your writing.

Whether you're describing a character in fiction, a very real person who's the subject of an article, the surroundings in which your action (fictional or true) is taking place, or a significant object that figures into the story, use good description that lets your readers feel, see, hear, smell, or taste.

Try your hand at some good descriptive sentences and paragraphs. Don't concentrate on describing just how things or people look, but include descriptions that involve the other four senses as well.

Valuable to any writer, the five senses are worth a lot more than five cents.

SENTENCES ARE NOT MEAT

When I was a kid, meat didn't come pre-wrapped in the supermarket. Instead, there was a butcher counter at the market; you stood in line to be waited on, and when it was your turn, the butcher cut or ground your meat to order. For hamburger meat, he sold us "chopped chuck." Now, chopping may be a fine thing to do to meat—we got many delicious hamburgers from Morty the butcher—but chopping is not such a wonderful thing to do to sentences.

Are your sentences choppy? Are they all short? Do you write lots of sentences that length? Do you fail to vary the length? Do you keep them all brief? Do you write lots of paragraphs as boring as this one?

On the other hand, sentences aren't Silly Putty either—they're not designed to be stre-e-e-etched out as long as you can possibly make them. Run-on sentences and grammatically correct but endless sentences are the opposite extreme. They're a flaw as serious as choppy sentences.

An occasional short sentence is no crime. By varying your sentences' length, you keep your writing flavorful and keep your reader interested. Also, a short sentence can be purposely used for impact. A short sentence in the midst of longer ones, or following one long one, packs a punch. It delivers impact. Here's an example:

The stage manager struggled in vain to lower the curtain, but no matter how he fought with it, the rope wouldn't move and the curtain wouldn't budge. Suddenly, down it came.

One short sentence packs a wallop—as you can see, in the paragraph above. But a steady diet of them would leave you (or your reader) feeling you were back in second grade.

Needlessly too-short sentences, along with run-on sentences, are only some of the problems you'll find in the following poorly written story. Rewrite it, improving it. An improved version follows, though it is by no means the only "right answer." There are a few out-and-out grammatical errors in the first version of the story, which have been corrected in the improved version. As far as the rest, however—making the sentences better lengths, making them flow more smoothly, avoiding needless repetition—the solution I've offered is only a suggestion.

Read the first version, then stop. Try your hand at improving the story before you read my revised version. Afterward, compare your revision with mine.

A SCARY DAY (version 1)

I want to tell you about a scary day. This scary day happened when I was in camp last summer. I was a C. I .T. last summer. A C. I .T. is a Counsellor in Training. The camp I go to lets it's campers come back as C.I.T.s when they're 16, so on account of I had just gotten to be 16 last June, I was allowed to be a C.I.T. in camp last summer, and what I was made a C.I.T. of was of horseback riding, which has always been my favorite thing of all in camp anyhow, ever since I was a little kid. I love horses and riding.

There was this mare named Sunshine. Sunshine is usually a very peaceful calm horse who, if she has any fault, it is that she doesn't want to trot when she's supposed to, but she'd just rather walk along slow no matter what. All right, Sunshine was in the ring. A kid named Jeff was riding her. Jeff was not too bad of a rider but not too good either, just kind of in-between. There were four other boys and girls in the ring at the time, too, on different other horses. I was in the ring on Trailblazer. She is a horse. Bobbie, the real regular riding counsellor, was outside the ring, trying to help some kid named Audrey adjust her stirrups, she was having a problem.

Trailblazer obeys me good. Audrey was riding a horse named Pickles. Bobbie asked me to watch the kids in the ring while she adjusted Audrey's stirrups. She asked me to have them walk and trot.

All of a sudden, Sunshine took off, I mean just jumped the fence and started running! I don't know what made her do it. Maybe a bee stung her. That was the best we could figure out, later on. It certainly wasn't like her.

I looked back, and saw Bobbie had her back to the ring, hadn't seen what had happened, and wasn't even on a horse. I decided I had to chase after Jeff and Sunshine. I yelled at Marcy, who was another kid who was in the ring. I yelled for her to tell Bobbie. Then I galloped off after Jeff and Sunshine. I just hoped Trailblazer was as good at jumping fences as Sunshine was, and that I would still be in the saddle when she landed on the other side of the fence.

I chased Sunshine all through the woods. I followed the little path. I kept being afraid I was going to see Jeff lying on the ground somewhere. I hoped that Trailblazer would stop in time if he was. Then I saw a fork in the path and didn't know which way to go. I gave Trailblazer her head. She took the left fork. I hoped she knew what she was doing. A little farther on we found Jeff, he had been thrown from Sunshine and was lying on the ground but he didn't look too bad, more scared than anything I think. I asked Jeff where it hurt. I knew not to move someone with a broken back, or even a broken leg if you didn't know what you were doing. He seemed mostly OK, crying hard but I think more from fear than hurt, so I decided I'd better get him back to camp and I helped him up on Trailblazer, which he was scared to do, and then I got up too.

I've never ridden two on a saddle but I've seen it in the movies. We met Bobbie when we were part of the way back, and she took Jeff from me and to the infirmary. Later she went out looking for Sunshine. Nothing was broken, just a lot of scrapes and bruises and a twisted ankle.

For two weeks nobody but Bobbie rode Sunshine, we were all afraid. But she behaved herself for the rest of the summer. I got a special award from the camp for bravery. I am going back next summer. Bobbie will too. Jeff isn't. I still love horses.

OK, here's one way to improve it:

29

A SCARY DAY (revision)

I don't think I've ever been as scared as I was one day last summer, in camp. Having turned 16 last June, I was eligible to be a Counsellor In Training, or C.I.T. I was happy to be assigned to help the riding counsellor. Riding was always my favorite activity in camp.

One of the horses we had at camp was a mare named Sunshine. Sunshine is usually a very peaceful, calm horse. If she has any fault, it's that she doesn't like to trot when she's supposed to. She prefers to just walk.

On the day I want to tell you about, a kid named Jeff was riding Sunshine around the ring. Jeff was an average rider, not particularly good or bad. Four other boys and girls were also riding in the ring at the time.

I was on a horse named Trailblazer. At the moment, Bobbie was outside the ring, trying to help a girl named Audrey adjust her stirrups. Audrey was having a problem with them. While Bobbie adjusted the stirrups, she asked me to watch the kids in the ring and have them walk and trot.

All of a sudden, Sunshine took off. For no apparent reason, she just jumped the fence and started running! I don't know why. Later, we decided that maybe a bee had stung her. That was the only explanation we could think of. It certainly wasn't like Sunshine to take off like that!

Looking back, I saw that Bobbie had her back to the ring and didn't realize what had happened. She wasn't even on a horse. I decided I had to chase after Jeff and Sunshine myself. A girl named Marcy, who was riding in the ring, was within yelling distance. I called to her to tell Bobbie that I was chasing a runaway horse. Then I galloped off after Jeff and Sunshine.

I just hoped Trailblazer was as good at jumping fences as Sunshine was, and that I would still be in the saddle when she landed on the other side of the fence.

We jumped safely, and I chased Sunshine all through the woods, following the little path.

As I rode, I kept worrying that I'd see Jeff lying on the ground somewhere. If he was, I hoped that Trailblazer would stop in time and not step on him. Then I saw a fork in the path. I didn't know which way to go, but I gave Trailblazer her head, and she took the left fork. I hoped she knew what she was doing.

A little farther on we found Jeff. He'd been thrown from Sunshine and was lying on the ground, but he didn't look too badly injured. He seemed more scared than anything. I asked Jeff where it hurt. I knew you're not supposed to move someone with a broken back, or even a broken leg if you don't know what you're doing.

Jeff seemed not to be too badly hurt, though. He was crying hard, but I think that was more from fear than pain, so I decided I'd better get him back to camp. I helped him up on Trailblazer. He was scared to mount a horse after having just been thrown from one, but he let me boost him up. Then I got up too. I'd never ridden two on a saddle, but I've seen it in the movies.

We met Bobbie when we were part of the way back, and she took Jeff from me and brought him to the infirmary. Nothing was broken. He just had a lot of scrapes and bruises and a twisted ankle.

Later, Bobbie went out looking for Sunshine. For two weeks after that, nobody but Bobbie rode that horse. The rest of us were afraid. But Sunshine behaved herself for the rest of the summer. I got a special award from the camp for bravery.

I'm going back to camp next summer, and Bobbie's returning too. I hope I can assist her again; I still love horses. Jeff isn't going back, which is no surprise to any of us.

JANE IS BORING

See Jane read. Jane reads fine. Jane reads easily. Jane's sentences are boring. Jane's sentences are repetitious. Jane's sentences are short. That is not the only problem. Most of Jane's sentences start with the subject.

I've already talked about varying sentence length for variety. (See "Sentences Are Not Meat," above) There are other ways, too, though, to give your sentence structure variety. The chief one is to avoid starting all your sentences with the subject.

As an example, take the following sentence: "Dan swung effortlessly and connected with a hard-pitched fastball that smacked dead-solid against his bat." It's not a short, choppy Dick-and-Jane sentence, but it does begin with a subject and continue immediately with a verb. Too many sentences in a row that follow the same structure will give your writing a boring, repetitive, even sing-song flavor.

How else could you construct that sentence?

Swinging effortlessly, Dan connected with a hard-pitched fastball that smacked dead-solid against his bat.

Effortlessly, Dan swung and connected with a hard-pitched fastball that smacked dead-solid against his bat.

Smack! Dan's bat connected dead-solid with the hard-pitched fastball as he swung effortlessly.

As he swung effortlessly, Dan's bat connected dead-solid with the hard-pitched fastball.

None of those sentences begins with the subject. In fact, each one begins with a different part of speech. Which brings me to the next point: Merely substituting verb-first sentences for subject-first sentences won't help. If all the sentences start with a verb, you're right back where you started: Boring. Repetitive. Contrived-sounding. What you need is to vary the structure.

At first, you'll need to make a conscious effort. It's a natural thing to start a sentence with the subject. Most sentences are about someone or something. It's only logical and natural to start by naming that person or thing, then saying what he did, or what it is doing, or what she is going to do.

Dan swung the bat. Jane will go to visit her aunt on Saturday. The weather is sunny. Spring is my favorite time of year.

And probably most sentences should start with the subject—but not all of them. Eventually, you'll find yourself varying your pattern naturally, without having to think about it. Till that time, give conscious thought to the order of your sentences.

Now try your hand at reconstructing the sentences below. Without using any word order that sounds forced, stilted, or unnatural, how many different ways can you rewrite these sentences?

Bob climbed the ladder but hit his head when he reached the ceiling.

Joey's homework was a real mess because his pen had leaked, and the teacher refused to accept it.

Sara talked to Jessica on the phone while she washed the dinner dishes.

Now write ten original sentences, none of which begins with the subject.

Finally, write a paragraph of at least five sentences. Vary the structure of the sentences so not all of them begin with the subject. Do not, however, start all of them with the verb instead, or use any structure that sounds forced or unnatural.

LOOK WHO'S TALKING!

In any argument, there are always at least two points of view, depending on how many people are involved. (Someone wise once said, "In any argument there are three points of view—yours, mine, and the truth." But that's a discussion for a different book.)

In writing fiction, too, there can be more than one point of view, although in most cases only one point of view is presented in any one story or book.

Point of view? Yes—who's telling the story? One of the characters? And if so, which one? Or should it be told from the point of view of an outside narrator, the writer of the story?

Although there are other viewpoints you'll find in books and stories on occasion, the three most common viewpoints are called first person, omniscient, and limited third person. What do these terms mean?

First-person viewpoint is just what the name sounds like. What are the first-person pronouns in grammar? I, we, me, us, my, our, mine, ours. And fiction told in the first person is told from the point of view of one person, one of the characters in the book or story: "I knew something was wrong as soon as I woke up, but it took me a minute to realize that my room was filled with smoke." That's an example of first person.

Fiction in the omniscient viewpoint is told in the third person, by the writer. The writer is not a part of the action, not a character in the story. He knows every character's thoughts and can describe actions happening in two different locations at the same time. ("Omniscient" means "all-knowing.") "Bob knew something was wrong as soon as he woke up, but it took him a minute to realize that his room was filled with smoke. That same morning, at the time Bob was waking up, his friend Danny was having an equally scary experience."

Limited third person refers to fiction also told by an outside narrator. In this case, however, the narrator can get into only one character's thoughts and only describes events that person is aware of. The action is all told in the third person: "Liz sanded down her bookcase, pouring out all her anger at Jackie's deception in the furious, circular strokes of the sandpaper." Nonetheless, despite the fact that the narrative is third person, if Liz doesn't know it or see it, neither does the reader.

What are the advantages to each?

First-person viewpoint gives the story much more immediacy. That is, it brings the reader closer to the story, allows him to get right into the thoughts and feelings and actions of that character. It makes him feel like he's part of the action.

On the other hand, it eliminates the possibility of the reader learning certain things. For instance, let's say the story concerns Bob's efforts to get onto the football team. Let's also assume that one of the plot's complications involves Bob's brother's car accident. The accident takes place while Bob is at the team's tryouts. If you tell the story in the first person from Bob's point of view, you cannot show the accident happening, since Bob wasn't present at the time of the accident.

You can keep the story in the first person and have Bob learn about the accident later, of course. His mom can tell him about it when he gets home, or he can walk past the scene and see his brother's wrecked car still sitting in the intersection. But if the crash is important to the story, and you want to show it happening, you cannot tell the story through Bob's eyes. He didn't see the crash. He was elsewhere at the time.

What are your choices? Basically you have two options. One is to keep the story in the first person but choose a different viewpoint character to tell it— someone who is present at the scene of the crash. The other is to choose the omniscient viewpoint.

The writer as omniscient narrator is privileged to know everything that's is going on. You can describe what occurs at the football field and also describe the car wreck, which is taking place at the same time, across town. Bob can't do that. He didn't see the car wreck.

His brother, in the wrecked car, can't describe what's happening at the football field. But you, as omniscient narrator, can describe both.

Similarly, you as omniscient narrator can get into the heads of more than one person. If Bob is telling the story, he can describe his own thoughts, hopes, fears, and other emotions and concerns. But he cannot speak for his brother, his mother, or any other character. He can know what they have told him they are feeling or thinking, but he cannot get into their heads to know what thoughts and feelings are really in there. You, as omniscient narrator, are privileged to know what's going on in the heads and hearts of all your characters.

If you decide on first-person viewpoint, how do you choose which character should tell the story? Usually the protagonist—the hero or heroine of the story—is your best choice. Usually, but not always. Sometimes a best friend, sister, or other person who's actively involved in what's happening may be a better choice as narrator.

There are various reasons for this. One is that this other person—let's say Bob's best buddy—is present during a crucial event in the story that occurs when Bob is somewhere else. This event is going to affect Bob very strongly, but he's not there when it happens. His friend who is there may be the best person to tell the story.

Another reason for choosing someone other than the protagonist as the viewpoint character is the character's attitude. Perhaps Bob has no faith in himself as a football player, but his best friend does. Bob's defeatist attitude might be too negative. It might make the story less enjoyable. It might even make the readers like him less.

On the other hand, his best friend might have much more faith in him. "I always knew Bob could make the team," his friend might start out by saying. Which sounds more like a story you'd want to read—one told by negative-thinking Bob, or one told by his optimistic best friend?

Yet another reason: You can be more candid about the protagonist. Suppose Bob is a really super person, and you need to convey this. If you have Bob talk about his volunteer work with needy kids, all the nice things he's done for his little brother, and the other things that make him so likeable, he may come off sounding conceited instead.

In a book, you might be able to show him doing all these things and get the message across to your reader that way. In a story, however, you probably don't have time to wander away from the main action. You don't have enough space to show Bob doing the many different things that will give your reader the idea you want to convey.

You can try to show Bob's good qualities through conversation. People talking to him can express their opinions about him. But sometimes there's no opportunity to work such conversations into the story in a way that doesn't sound forced or artificial. Another problem: All that talking will take up valuable space. It may also slow down the action.

What's the answer? Tell the story from his best buddy's point of view. You can't have Bob saying, "I really deserved to win that award! I'm one of the nicest people I know!" How nice can he be if he's that egotistical? But his best buddy can easily say, "If they ever start handing out awards for all-around nice guy at Jefferson High, I'm going to see to it that Bob gets nominated. In fact, I think he could win the all-state title."

On the other hand, suppose your story is about an anti-hero. Your protagonist is an unpleasant character who gets what's coming to him in the end, or undergoes a transformation, as Scrooge does in A Christmas Carol.

Chances are, he doesn't see himself as others see him. The whole town may hate him, you may hate him, and you probably want your readers to hate him too. But it's

37

likely that Bob doesn't hate himself. He probably thinks he has a perfectly good reason for all his nasty actions. So he's not going to start out the story by saying, "I'll bet I'm the meanest, nastiest, most awful person who ever attended Columbus Junior High."

Once again, if you're writing a story, rather than a book, you probably don't have the luxury of showing him beating up a little kid for his lunch money, cheating on his finals, and blaming poor innocent Seth for dumping yellow paint all over Pete Havermyer's new car. You have to get the message across in a couple of quick sentences—and they probably can't come from Bob and sound natural. But if there's a character who knows what Bob's been up to, and what he's really like, a character who's involved in all the action in the book, consider having him be your narrator, even though Bob is your protagonist.

Another reason for having a different viewpoint character than the protagonist is a secret. No, I don't mean I'm keeping the reason a secret from you. I mean that the protagonist might possess some knowledge that you want to keep a secret from the reader.

If the story is told from Bob's viewpoint, it may not be possible to keep that information from coming out earlier than you want the reader to know it. (If you do manage to keep Bob from revealing it, it's possible that the reader will scream "Unfair!" at the end.) But if the story is told by Bob's best friend, or any other character who doesn't have that information, the reader won't learn it too early either.

Still another reason for having someone other than the protagonist as the viewpoint character is if the protagonist's life is in danger. Perhaps Bob, the protagonist, is a detective who gets into a high-risk situation; or maybe he is a man with a serious illness. If Bob is telling the story, the reader can logically conclude that the villain's bullet will miss him, that he is going to recover from double pneumonia, that that he will duck whatever other dangers he is facing. It removes some of the tension from the story, and you, the writer, don't want to lose that tension. So have someone else tell the story instead of Bob and keep the reader worrying.

Now, supposing Bob, our hero, has an enemy named Burt plotting against him, but Bob is totally unaware of Burt's plans. If you want the reader to worry his way through the story, the reader must be aware of Burt's schemes. If you tell the story through Bob's eyes, you have no way for your reader to learn of the plot against him. Only by telling the story through Burt's eyes can you convey the information your reader needs—assuming you are determined to tell this story in the first person.

Of course, many of the situations I've just described can be handled by telling the story in the omniscient viewpoint. You, the writer, can certainly tell the reader what a wonderful or awful person Bob is, or just what danger is lurking around the corner, for instance. But if you've decided that you want to tell this story in the first person, a narrator other than your protagonist is called for.

There's a variation on first-person viewpoint that doesn't get used very often.

Multiple first-person is just what its name implies: More than one person tells the story. It's very rare to find this type of viewpoint in a story; even in books, you don't find it often. One way to work it is to have alternating chapters, one from Bob's point of view and the next from Danny's, then Bob's again, and so on.

Another way this is accomplished is by having Janet tell the story but also having her read excerpts from Luanne's diary, or having her receive letters from Luanne. Most of the story is from Janet's viewpoint, but the diary excerpts or letters are from Luanne's viewpoint.

Assignment: Briefly rewrite any first-person story you are familiar with, so that it's told in third person instead. It can even be a brief retelling of a book. Now do the same in reverse: Take a third-person story you're familiar with and rewrite it in first person.

Now experiment with different first-person viewpoints. Write a scene describing an argument between an older sister and a younger brother, who fight in front of their mother. First write the scene from the brother's point of view. Now write it again from the mother's point of view.

One more exercise: Choose an ordinary object— perhaps an ice cream cone, although you can choose a different object if you prefer. Now have three different people talk about it and describe it: A toothless man of 85, a seven-year-old boy, and the woman who owns the ice cream store.

The point of this last exercise is to make you more aware of the differences in speech, in perception, and in description between three different people. When you write in the first person, you need to make your viewpoint character believable. If he's a 10-year-old boy, he needs to talk like a 10-year-old boy and think like a 10-year-old boy. If she's an overly strict mom, then that's what she has to sound like.

JUST THE FACTS, MA'AM

In the '50s, '60s, and '70s, first on radio and then on TV, there was a police drama called "Dragnet." (The show still pops up sometimes on cable TV.) Even today, people quote detective Joe Friday, who, with his partner, solved a crime every week. His famous request, spoken to the victims and witnesses he interviewed, was "Just the facts, ma'am."

Friday might as well have been a reporter, instead of a cop. Today there's a growing trend among some reporters to use fiction techniques in reportorial writing. (See "It Was a Dark and Stormy Story.") But still, in a great number of factual articles, whether for newspapers or certain magazines, the facts are all you want. No opinion, and very little extraneous description.

Some description, however, can be suitable even in a facts-only article. For instance: "On a calm, sunny afternoon last week, the benign weather gave no hint that matters downtown were anything but placid. But inside the governmental offices last Wednesday, the mood was definitely at odds with the calm and cheery day." After you grab the reader's interest with your lead, though, you need to know when to stick to facts.

Straight news is straight news. It isn't fiction. It isn't even an opinion piece. And if you're writing for a publication that doesn't appreciate a fiction-style lead, or if you're writing to fit a lot of words into a tight space, or if you're writing for a publication with a stick-to-the-facts style, you'd better know how to deliver what the editor wants.

You may plan on being a poet or novelist, an essayist or lyricist, an ad copywriter or some other type of writer than newspaper or magazine reporter. But life is funny; we don't always wind up where we think we're going.

The late and sorely missed columnist Lewis Grizzard didn't start out intending to be a humorist. His interest lay in sports; he thought his future lay in sportswriting. That was where he started, all right, but his career path took an unexpected—and delightful—turn.

So might yours. Or you might find yourself working on a community weekly newspaper as a teenager, to get some valuable writing experience. Even if you never write a single piece of reportorial writing, learning to write tightly and concisely is a skill that will stand you in good stead in any kind of writing.

Assignment: Write an article of 300 words or less, in straight reportorial style, on any recent event in your school, your family, or your neighborhood. Use any type of lead you want, but then stick strictly to the facts, making sure all the important ones get included. Remember the "five Ws" discussed earlier in this book: Who, What, Where, When, and Why.

EXERCISE IN DESCRIPTIONS—AND MORE

When writing fiction, you need to get to know your characters. If you're writing a book, you need to know them very well. Even for a short story, you want to know more about them than just what the reader learns in the course of the story. There are many novelists who write complete profiles of all their major characters before they set a word of the actual book down on paper.

Here are some things you may want to know about your main characters. Not everything on the list is essential, and you may think of other items you'd like to add, so feel free to add to the list, or drop an item or two: Name, nickname, age, appearance, hobbies, interests, pet hates and pet peeves, occupation (or, if the character is still a student, career plans), how much education he has had, important family members, pets, favorite kind of music, favorite foods, favorite sports, favorite books, favorite color, and biggest fears.

Some of these facts will turn out to be important to the plot, or at least to your descriptions of the characters. Others will never be mentioned in the book, but knowing them will help you get a better feel for who your characters are. And when you know who they are, and what their backgrounds are, you'll be able to have them act in more believable ways. Also, the words you put in their mouths will sound both more realistic and more distinctive.

Take Ron and Luke, two fictional characters, for example. Ron is a painfully shy 15-year-old boy who's never had a date, whose pets are snakes, who gets straight As, who's no good at sports, and who desperately wants to be popular. Luke is the immensely popular president of a college fraternity, whose hobby is raising show dogs, who maintains a B average only through very hard work, is a passable basketball and football player even though he's never tried out for the team, who comes from a rich family, and whose father was killed when Luke was 12. Ron and Luke are going to speak and act very differently from each other.

The more you know about your characters, the more believable their speech and actions will be.

As an exercise, cut out ten pictures from magazine ads (not pictures of recognizable, famous people). Now write at least a paragraph about each one.

Start by describing him or her physically. Include both items that you can actually see in the picture (eye color, hair color, and other attributes that are apparent) and items that you invent. ("He has a tattoo on his back. It's a snake. He got it on a dare one night when he was feeling rebellious. Now he hides it and never takes his shirt off, not even at the beach.")

Also describe the person in other terms than his appearance. Mostly, this part of the description will come straight out of your imagination, but some of it may be suggested by something in the picture. If the picture is of a very thin woman, you might decide that she is anorexic but getting treatment for the condition. If the picture is of a sloppily dressed man, you might decide that he's a slob and leaves his clothes strewn around the house, his dinner dishes piled in the sink, and his garbage can overflowing.

Tell as much about the person as you care to: Where he lives, what he does for a living, whom he lives with, and so forth. You can include as many details as you'd like. Even such things as what he named his pet will tell something about him. (What would you assume about a person who calls his dog "Fido" or "Rover"?

What would you assume about a person who names a tiny chihuahua "Killer," or a spotted dog "Stripe"? Is a dull, unimaginative, plodding, methodical sort of person likely to name his cat "Archimedes" or "Zoltan"?)

ARE YOU A "PASSIVIST"?

Of course, a person who's anti-war, or who attempts to promote peace between fighting friends, is a pacifist. But if you write sentences like the following, you may be labelled a "passivist": "The leaf was tossed by the wind," "The cat was chased by the dog," or "My brother was sent to his room by my mom."

What's wrong with those sentences? Technically, nothing. That is, gramatically they're correct. But they're all written in the passive voice. The subject of each sentence (leaf, cat, brother) is the recipient of the action, not the person or thing doing the action. A sentence is much more forceful, carries much more impact, and makes your writing much stronger if it's written in the active voice.

Not "Someone had something done to them," but "Someone did something." It's better to write, "The wind tossed the leaf," "The dog chased the cat," and "My mom sent my brother to his room." (Notice, too, that the active sentences take up fewer words to say the same thing than the passive sentences.)

A good rule in writing is to use the active voice rather than the passive. There are a few instances where the passive might be preferable, but they are very few, for sure.

Assignment: To make yourself more aware of the two voices, and which one you're using, write ten sentences in the passive voice, then rewrite them in the active voice.

REPORTERS AREN'T CATS

Curiosity killed the cat. Isn't it lucky you aren't feline! You can ask and ask, and you won't get killed. In fact, if you don't ask the right questions in an interview, you won't get a good story out of it.

When interviewing someone, it's a good idea to bring along a recorder. First, the recorder will capture the person's answers more accurately than you can by taking notes. Second, you won't have to say, "Slow down! I can't write that fast!" and maybe interrupt the interviewee's flow of thought.

Third, if there's ever any dispute about what the interviewee said, and there are accusations that you've misquoted, a recording is undeniable evidence of what was actually said. Fourth, if you don't have to busy yourself with writing everything the interviewee says, you can be free to look at the interviewee and her surroundings.

Make notes about what you observe. Does she frown a lot? Is she nervously tapping her toes or fingers throughout much of the conversation? What does she look like? What is her house or office like? If you're interviewing someone for an article about him, his appearance, demeanor (whether he's calm, agitated, brusque, or impatient, for instance), voice, and surroundings are all relevant.

Look around. Listen not only to the words but the tone of voice. Make notes on everything. If the interview is of a no-nonsense businesswoman, and she's got a collection of china dolls on a curio shelf in her office, that's certainly an interesting contrast that is worth reporting on.

Even if it's a different kind of interview, it pays to observe. Suppose you're interviewing the principal of your school for the school newspaper. You're writing an article on discipline problems in Edgewater Junior High.

It's not a profile of the principal himself, so perhaps such details as the award certificate hanging on the wall aren't important.

But there are other details you'll be free to observe if you aren't having to keep your eyes glued to a notepad. And those details can not only add color to your article but also open up other areas of questioning. Does the principal tap a pencil on the desk impatiently when discussing the number of knives removed from students in the last month? Is there a bulging green folder labelled DISCIPLINE INFRACTIONS on his desk that's conspicuous for its size? If you're free to notice these details, you'll have the opportunity to think of other questions to ask:

"You seem agitated over the question of knives. Are weapons a particular problem in this school?"

"I see you have a large folder labelled DISCIPLINE INFRACTIONS. How many were there last year? How many this year, so far? What is the single biggest category of discipline problems in this school? Is that true throughout the district?"

Go to your interview with a prepared set of questions...but always be ready to change course and ask others that aren't on your list. If something you see or hear during the interview suggests an additional question, or a whole new area of questions, don't be afraid to deviate from the ones you've prepared.

Ask about what you've seen or heard while interviewing the person. Follow up on anything she's said that intrigued you. If it raised a new question in your mind, chances are your readers will be wondering too.

Whenever possible, ask open-ended questions, rather than yes-or-no questions. Of course, some yes-or-no questions are inevitable. "Are you planning on running for student council president again next year?" is a perfectly fine inquiry. But for a profile of someone—say, the town mayor—"Tell me about your childhood," or the more narrowly focussed, "What is your happiest childhood memory?" will elicit a much broader, more informative answer than "Did you have a happy childhood?"

Be a good listener. Don't be afraid to jump in with another question, but do be sure your interviewee has finished answering the last question, first. Sometimes someone has just paused for a breath, or to think how to phrase an answer.

And if you feel the person isn't answering your question, either because she's evading it or because she didn't understand it, rephrase the question and try again: "No, what I wanted to know was _____." Or, "But I still don't know _____?"

Assignment: Practice your interviewing techniques on your family—parents, grandparents, or other relatives. You may not have anyone famous in the family, but that doesn't mean none of them is worth interviewing. Has any of your relatives done anything interesting in his or her life?

Perhaps one of them at one time had an occupation that no longer exists because of modern technology. Interview him about his past job, career, or profession. Did one of your relatives emigrate from another country? Interview her about life in "the old country," and how it differed from life in this country as it was when she arrived here.

Is one of your relatives at least two generations older than you—a grandparent, great-aunt, or great-uncle, or a cousin of your grandparents' generation? Interview him on the differences between life in his childhood, or his young adulthood, and now. The article that results can probably run in your school newspaper.

I'll bet there are plenty of kids in your school who don't realize there was a time when, if you picked up the phone, you heard, not a dial tone, but an operator asking, "Number please?" (For that matter, if your friends your age have grown up with cell phones, they

47

may not even know what a dial tone is!) And what did your grandparents, who had no video games, do for fun when their homework was finished? How about your great-grandparents, who had no TV either? What other modern conveniences didn't exist in these relatives' childhoods or young adulthoods? In what other way was life different then?

Make up a list of questions...but be prepared to ask additional ones. Some of your interviewee's replies will raise other questions in your mind. You can be sure some of your readers will have those same questions in their minds, too.

Even if the article you write never gets published, it will be good practice for your interviewing technique.

AVOID THESE LIKE THE PLAGUE

As that wonderful writer on language, William Safire, once said, "Avoid clichés like the plague." Cliches are expressions that have been used too often—like "Avoid it like the plague," or "He's strong as an ox." Other examples of clichés include "few and far between," "last but not least," "I'd bet my bottom dollar," "he can't see the forest for the trees," "he left her high and dry," and "she left no stone unturned."

It's impossible to avoid clichés altogether, but a good writer uses them sparingly. There are times when it's appropriate to use a cliché. Sometimes there's no better way to say what you want to. Sometimes you'll use one on purpose because it's appropriate in the context of what you're saying. For instance, if you were writing about a company that wiped out a whole section of a forest to harvest lumber, it would be very appropriate to use the cliché about not seeing the forest for the trees.

Assignment: Make a list of as many clichés as you can. Now that you're more aware of them, make an effort to avoid using such trite expressions in your writing.

AS COLD AS THE PRINCIPAL'S HEART

A good simile is as useful to a writer as a potholder is to a cook with a roast in the oven. If it's well crafted, it can be as beautiful as the sun setting over a tropical horizon. (In case you didn't realize it, I have just used two similes to make my point.)

A simile is a descriptive comparison, like the two I used in the paragraph above. It uses "like" or "as" in the comparison. If you leave out the "like" or "as," then the comparison is called a metaphor. An example of a metaphor is, "Her wind-blown red hair was a wildly dancing flame."

A good simile or metaphor is one that's easily understandable to the reader. At the same time, it shouldn't rely on an image that's been used so often that it has become a cliché. For instance, "black as crows at midnight" is certainly descriptive. Most people will get a pretty good mental image from the phrase. But "black as crows at midnight" has been used so often that it's become a cliché.

"Black as pitch" is another simile that's been around for a long time. It's a bad choice for two reasons. Not only is it clichéd, but it's probably not meaningful to many people anymore. Pitch? To most people, pitch is what a particular baseball player does; or it refers to how high or low your voice is. It's also a coal tar residue, but how many people today know that. Did you? That definition of the word is meaningless to many people. The simile, as a result, falls flat.

Instead of such clichés, try to think of new similes. Instead of the overused "limp as a dishrag," say "limp as a flag on a windless day."

Other overworked similes include "Pure as the

driven snow," "soft as a kiss," and "white like the Arctic."
See if you can think of more original similes for "pure,"
"white," and "soft."

Now think of 10 other similes...and, while you're at
it, 10 metaphors as well.

POETRY

Poetry is a distinct area of writing, and many
people write all their lives without ever committing
a poem to paper. But even if your interests lie in the
direction of fiction, humorous essays, or some other
distinctly non-poetic form of writing, it's good to have
a grasp of some of the basics. As I said earlier in this
book, you never know what you're going to wind up writing,
despite what you think now...or what you may think 10
years from now.

Poetry is divided into rhymed and unrhymed verse,
metered and free verse. If that sounds complicated, I'll
uncomplicate it for you quickly:

Rhymed verse is poetry in which the sounds at
the ends of some or all of the lines rhyme according to a
regular pattern. I'll discuss those patterns in a couple of
minutes.

Unrhymed verse is poetry in which there is no
attempt made to rhyme any of the lines. In fact, the poet
may make a conscious effort to be sure that none of the
lines rhyme. If two lines rhyme, it sets the reader up to
expect more rhymes.

Metered verse, whether or not it rhymes, follows
a certain rhythm. The lines may all sound like this, for
instance: Dah-DAH, dah-DAH, dah-DAH, dah-DAH. That's
one kind of meter; there are others. I'll discuss the
various kinds of meter in a couple of minutes.

Free verse can have a line made up of two words,
followed by a line made up of 10 words. It doesn't follow a

set meter, so it might sound like Dah-DAH-dah, dah-DAH, DAH-dah, dah-dah-DAH. It almost reads as if someone took a paragraph of prose (prose is the opposite of poetry) and broke it up into lines so it looks like a poem. But a true free verse poem has a hard-to-define poetic quality about it. When you read it aloud, even though it isn't metered and probably doesn't rhyme, it still sounds like a poem.

Now let's look at rhyme schemes. There are many. Some depend on multiple verses and involve such tricks as the last line of each verse rhyming with the last line of all the other verses. Or you might have a six-line verse, with the first and third lines rhyming with each other, the second and fourth lines rhyming with each other, and the fifth and sixth lines rhyming with each other. But let's talk about four-line verses—the most usual length—and the most common rhyme schemes for four-line verses.

Those rhyme schemes have names: ABAB, ABCB, ABBA, and AABB. What do they mean? The letters refer to the sound that ends the line. The sound that ends the first line is referred to as "A." The next, different, sound to end a line is referred to as "B." If there's a third one, it's called "C." Another would be "D" and so on.

ABAB is a rhyme scheme in which the first and third lines rhyme with each other, and the second and fourth lines rhyme with each other. A very simple verse of poetry that illustrates the ABAB rhyme scheme is:

My dog is white.
His name is Spot.
He's loud all night.
He barks a lot.

Now, that poem is not going to win any prizes, but it does serve to illustrate the ABAB rhyme scheme.

ABCB is a rhyme scheme in which the second and fourth lines rhyme with each other, but the first and third lines don't rhyme with anything.

My dog is white.

His name is Spot.
I love him though
He barks a lot.

In the ABBA rhyme scheme, as you can probably guess by now, the first and fourth lines rhyme with each other, and the second and third lines rhyme with each other.

My dog's named Spot.
His coat is white.
He barks all night.
Mom yells a lot.

And in AABB, of course, the first and second lines rhyme with each other, and the third and fourth lines rhyme with each other.

My dog's named Spot.
He barks a lot.
His fur is rough
And he is tough.

Meter is the rhythm of the poem's lines. Do they all sound like dah-DAH, dah-DAH, dah-DAH, dah-DAH? That's called iambic poetry. Each dah-DAH is called an iamb. If, instead, the poem sounds like DAH-dah, DAH-dah, DAH-dah, DAH-dah, it's trochaic. One DAH-dah is called a trochee. Dah-dah-DAH, dah-dah-DAH, dah-dah-DAH, dah-dah-DAH is anapestic poetry; one dah-dah-DAH is an anapest. And DAH-dah-dah, DAH-dah-dah, DAH-dah-dah, DAH-dah-dah is dactyllic poetry. One DAH-dah-dah is a dactyll.

There's an old rhyme that's useful for remembering which kind of meter a poem has:

The iamb saunters through my book,
Trochees rush and tumble.
While the anapest runs like a hurrying brook,
Dactylls are stately and classical.

Each iamb, trochee, anapest, or dactyll, by itself, is called a foot (although you'll never find one wearing shoes—and it's not made up of 12 inches, either).

You don't need to memorize the terms that follow, but here are some you may want to know: Poetry made up of one foot to the line (although it's very rare) is called monometer. Poems composed of two feet to the line are dimeter. A three-foot line is trimeter, a four-foot line is tetrameter, a five-foot line is pentameter, six is hexameter, seven is heptameter, and eight is octometer.

Many children's poems are written in tetrameter, though pentameter is said to be the most common in English poetry.

In some poems, the meter, or the number of feet per line, or both are not the same in every line. For instance, the first and third lines may be alike, but different from the second and fourth lines, which are like each other.

> White snow drifts down
> Soft and still.
> Draping ev'ry
> Graceful hill.

Not all poetry describes love, sunsets, or other topics often thought of as "poetic." What's known as "cowboy poetry" is rugged, masculine, and can deal with anything from faithful dogs to polluted rivers, or a variety of other subjects.

Rap music is a form of poetry. So are rock lyrics. Much satire and many parodies are written in poetic form. You may be familiar with the names of Mark Russell, the satirist who appeared with his piano on Public Broadcasting; Allan Sherman, the late parodist who had many hit record albums; or Tom Lehrer, whose parody and satire became famous through concerts and record albums.

Experiment with poetry. Try your hand at rhymed and unrhymed, metered and free verse. Play with different rhyme schemes. If you've never tried to write a song lyric before, and you're feeling adventurous, try that too.

53

PART TWO:

Other Kinds of Writing to Try

When you think of writing, you probably think mainly in terms of stories, articles, and books. Or perhaps your interests include writing poems and plays (or movie scripts). But there are lots of other forms of writing, some of which you can try your hand at right now.

Even if you think you know what kind of writing interests you, and what you intend to write in your future career, it's good to try your hand at other kinds of writing as well. At best, you might find an area that interests you even more than the science fiction novels or biographies you plan to write some day. At worst, even if you don't change your career plans, you'll still have gotten practice in another area of writing.

You may focus on fiction, then one day decide to collaborate with a friend on song lyrics. You may become a successful TV scriptwriter and eventually decide to write your autobiography. You could plan a career as a poet but find yourself paying the rent by writing advertisements. You could be a struggling novelist who, to supplement your income, takes a job writing the fortunes for a fortune-cookie company!

Here's another thing to consider: If you get a good feel for writing poetry, your fiction may have a poetic lilt to it. If you become a good fiction-writer, you'll be better able to write some of the fiction-style leads for nonfiction articles I discussed earlier. Proficiency at playwriting can lead to writing better dialogue in your fiction. There's no form of writing that doesn't at least have the potential to make you better at some other form of writing.

So try your hand at as many of the following writing projects as possible.

SLOGANS

Slogans such as you see on bumper stickers, or on the kind of large buttons you pin on, are very short statements. Yet in just a few words, they make a point, frequently with humor. Writing such slogans will give you practice in getting your point across in very few words.

Many slogans are for political or social causes: Save the Earth, Vote for Jones, Save the Whales, Impeach Smith, or Equal Rights for Lefthanded Mandolinists.

Slogan-writers know that, besides brevity, humor is helpful too, where possible. A little humor goes a long way toward getting the message across. It makes it easier to take. It makes it more memorable. (Some causes, of course, don't lend themselves to humor, and there is even less space on a button than there is on a bumper sticker, which limits the number of words to get funny in.)

What's true of buttons and bumper stickers holds true for many other kinds of writing as well: A little humor often helps get people's attention and helps get the point across. Humor, though, should not be forced. If humor doesn't come naturally to you, skip it.

BOYCOTT FUR-BEARING PEOPLE

FUR SHOULD BE WORN ON
THE ONES IT WAS BORN ON

These two slogans support the movement against killing animals in order to make fur coats. Whether or not you agree with the sentiment, you'll agree that both slogans get the point across with punch and humor.

A popular bumper sticker reads:

MY CHILD IS AN HONOR STUDENT AT _____ SCHOOL

But you may also have seen bumper stickers that read:

MY KID CAN BEAT UP YOUR HONOR STUDENT

I suspect that some of the people with the second bumper sticker may not even be parents with kids of school age. They're just tired of seeing that first bumper sticker. They have something to say, and some clever slogan-writer gave them the way to say it.

Of course, not all buttons and bumper stickers support causes or advertise the owner's beliefs. Some just promote the wearer of the button or driver of the car. Some promote the ethnic background of the owner. Some poke fun at other slogans. Some are just for fun.

KISS ME, I'M IRISH

IT'S TRUE—BLONDES HAVE MORE FUN

IF YOU CAN READ THIS BUMPER STICKER, YOU'RE TOO CLOSE

I BRAKE FOR PEOPLE

The person who thinks of the next good place to wear slogans, besides on buttons and bumper stickers, may get rich starting a new fad. Meanwhile, there are writers who actually make money (not big money, but money all the same) writing slogans for buttons and bumper stickers. Whether or not you're interested in writing such slogans in the future, please practice now. It's a good exercise in getting your point across with brevity, preferably with wit humor as well.

Think of as many slogans as you can that make a point, are short, punchy, and preferably humorous.

CREATIVE MENUS

Though many restaurants simply list the foods they offer, others describe their foods in as appealing and attractive a manner as possible. The restaurant's patrons' mouths water before they ever see or smell the food. The menu's descriptions alone are enough to do it.

For instance, instead of simply offering "Hamburger," the menu might read, "Juicy, lean, thick patty of prime sirloin, exquisitely seasoned with our secret spice and herb blend, perfectly char-broiled, and served with a luscious accompaniment of slices of Bermuda onion and red, vine-ripened tomato." Which of those two offerings will be more appealing to most people—the plain old hamburger, or the exquisitely seasoned, exquisitely described juicy patty?

Try describing some of your favorite foods as they might appear on an appealingly written menu. For fun, you may want to ask your mom what's for dinner one night, then write a menu listing and describing the foods she plans to serve.

REVIEWS: THE PEN IS MIGHTIER THAN THE SWORD

What do you think of an assignment that requires you to watch TV? If you're going to write a review of a TV program—and that's just what you're going to write next—then, of course, you have to see the program, first.

If you're not already familiar with the format

of a review, first you need to read several. Your local newspaper almost certainly offers reviews of TV shows, if not every day then perhaps on Sundays, or just from time to time. Read several and study them.

Notice the aspects of the TV show that are criticized. Usually these might include the writing, subject matter, actors' talent, suitability of actors for their roles, costumes, and directing. Other factors may also come in for consideration, such as special effects, or choice of time slot for the program. Reviews may be written in a clever, witty, or otherwise funny tone, or they may be straightforwardly informational with no attempt to inject humor.

Write a review of your favorite show. Now watch a program you wouldn't be likely to watch normally and write a review of it.

Of course, TV shows aren't the only things to get reviewed. Plays, movies, books, concerts, dance programs, and even artwork are subject to being criticized (or complimented) in print. Search through your local paper for reviews of other things besides TV shows (the Sunday edition may hold the most reviews), study them for format and content, and then write reviews of as many different things as you can.

If you've recently seen a show—even a local school's production of a play—you can review that. Seen a concert recently—even if it was a local band? How about a movie—whether you saw it in a theatre or on video? Got a new CD or MP3 or download? Review any or all of these. Then there are book reviews. These are not the same as book reports you write for English class. Again, study the newspaper, or a magazine that includes reviews, for the format of a professional review.

Notice in reading printed reviews that most reviews are short. They usually aren't allotted as much space as is given to a news article or feature story.

Just for fun—and more practice—why don't you

also write a review of:
- A comic book
- A line of greeting cards
- A cereal box with entertaining stuff printed on it
- A schoolbook
- A boxed game
- An instruction manual that came with something electronic, such as a TV, microwave oven, or boombox. Critique it on whatever makes an instruction manual good or bad: Is it clearly written and easy to understand? Is it well organized and presented in a logical order? If you have a question, is it easy to find the answer quickly? Are there lots of typographical errors in it? (Instruction manuals are notorious for typos.) Are there enough diagrams, if applicable, and are the diagrams well drawn?

Critics are powerful people. Theatre critics, giving a bad review to a show, can result in the show closing after just a few performances. TV critics who write bad reviews cause many people to turn to another channel. This can result in poor ratings, and ultimately in the show's being cancelled. Critics of other arts have similar power.

Critics can also, of course, direct an audience to a fabulous play, worthwhile TV show, good book, soaring ballet, melodious symphony, or dynamite rock group. If your local paper's critic, or a national critic in a magazine or on TV, writes a glowing review of a movie or TV show, the chances are better you'll go to see that movie or tune in that show.

Feel the power—write as many reviews as you want. The pen is truly mightier than the sword.

TECHNICAL WRITING

"Writing" often calls to mind lyrical descriptions of blue skies, detailed descriptions of people—characters—

and prose that often verges on being poetic. It's what's frequently called "creative writing."

In this section of the book, we're talking about other types of writing than those that are most commonly thought of when someone says "writing." In addition to novels, nonfiction books, and short stories and articles, "writing," as you're being reminded in this section, also encompasses ad-writing, menu-writing, greeting card-writing, and many other forms of the craft of putting words together well. But most of them still involve making your words attractive, your sentences descriptive, and your writing imaginative and appealing.

Then there's technical writing.

What is technical writing? Well, the form of technical writing you're probably most familiar with is software manuals. Whenever you buy software and read the accompanying book that tells you how to use it, you're reading technical writing. Instruction manuals that come with almost anything else, from an assemble-it-yourself bicycle to a home appliance, are another example of technical writing. And then of course, there are scientific articles or books, such as those detailing scientific discoveries or explaining new theories.

But instruction manuals or leaflets are the type of technical writing you're most likely to be familiar with... and the type you're most likely to write at some possible future time. There is a growing demand for technical writers.

Here you are not expected—or wanted—to describe the glowing beauty of the cold and shiny aluminum part in a device. All you need to do is explain how to use it, or how to assemble it—in clear and comprehensible language.

Here you are not expected to guess at the number of people who were needed in the manufacture of one small copper part. You are expected only to explain how to use that part in some technical process.

This is the exact opposite of ~~creative~~ writing: Leave out interesting descriptiveness. Don't go off on flights of fancy. Human interest isn't wanted here either. Just explain how to use, or how to assemble, the item this writing accompanies.

As an exercise, write a set of instructions for a procedure you're very familiar with. Please choose something that can't be explained in four easy steps. Remember to make your instructions clear and comprehensible. Remember not to assume that your reader has any prior knowledge of the subject. Start at the beginning and talk your reader through the procedure step by step, in logical order, using simple language.

You can choose instructions for doing something, for assembling something, or for some computer-related task.

Always keep your reader in mind. It may help if, while you write, you picture someone—perhaps someone you actually know, though not necessarily—and write as if you were explaining it to him or her. Assume he or she doesn't have any knowledge at all of what you are talking about. None.

Now try it.

LIMERICKS: THERE ONCE WAS A TALENTED TEEN

You may already recognize the meter in the subtitle above: It's the opening line of a limerick. A form of poem with a unique and specific structure, limericks have been popular for centuries. Though they are famous for often being a little risqué, many examples exist of limericks you could comfortably repeat to your grandmother. One classic limerick that will offend no one is:

An epicure dining at Crewe
Found quite a large mouse in the stew.

Said the waiter, "Don't shout
And wave it about,
Or the rest will be wanting one too."
The limerick above demonstrates more than just
the fact that clean limericks can be funny. It also
demonstrates the classic limerick rhyme scheme (AABBA)
and deviates only slightly from the classic limerick meter,
which is:

Dah-DAH-dah-dah-DAH-dah-dah-DAH
Dah-DAH-dah-dah-DAH-dah-dah-DAH
Dah-DAH-dah-dah-DAH
Dah-DAH-dah-dah-DAH
Dah-DAH-dah-dah-DAH-dah-dah-DAH

Here is the beginning of a limerick. You complete it:

A strange high school teacher, Miss Bloom,
Used to say to the kids in her room,

_____

_____

_____

Here's another for you to finish:

I once had a friend named Elaine.
This girl was a genuine pain.

_____

_____

_____

Now write one or more limericks from scratch.

ADVERTISEMENTS

You know what the purpose of an advertisement is,
of course: Ads are intended to make you want to buy a
particular product, or use a particular service (such as a
plumber, a lawyer, or a tutoring service), or to give money
to a certain charity or other cause (such as the Red Cross
or the United Way), or to vote for a certain candidate in
an election.

But have you ever given much thought to a radio or TV commercial, or an ad in print? When you watch TV, listen to the radio, or read a magazine, have you ever stopped to think about the ads? What is there about a particular ad that's supposed to make you want to buy the product—whether the product is peanut butter or a presidential candidate?

• Is it a straightforward commercial that praises the product and lists the benefits you'll get from it?

• Does it compare this brand with its competitors and tell you why this brand is better?

• Does it offer testimonials from experts, or from ordinary people who use the product and like it? Or from famous people who use it and like it? (Does the fact that someone is a famous actor or athlete mean that they really know which is the better brand of bologna, clothing, or car, or the better candidate for public office? Do people think famous people know better?)

• Does it work on you by trying to convince you that "everyone" has this product or buys this brand? That if you want to be part of the "in" crowd, you'll buy it too?

• Does it try to convince you—directly or indirectly—that you'll be a better or more popular person if you buy this product?

• Is it a particularly clever commercial, which tries to win you over with humor?

• Does it rely on technical brilliance, such as animation or special effects?

• Is it persuasive in some other way? How?

Now that you've studied commercials and ads to see how they try to persuade you, write some commercials yourself. Write at least one commercial each for:

• An existing real product you're personally familiar with. (Suggestions: a brand of soda, a video game, an amusement park, athletic shoes, your favorite fast-food restaurant or pizza joint.)

- An unpopular food item such as spinach, broccoli, or liver.
- A product you've just made up for the sake of this exercise.
- A candidate for office, either national or local. (If there are no election campaigns currently underway, write an ad for someone who might run in the next election.)
- A candidate for class president, student council president, or some other elected office in your school. (Again, if no election race is underway now, write an ad for someone who might possibly run in the future. And if your school doesn't have elections for such positions as student council president or class president, pretend it does.)
- A public service ad. This is an ad that doesn't sell a product but rather advises people that it's healthy to quit smoking, that only you can prevent forest fires, that this is National Safety Week, that you should donate blood, that you should register and vote, or that you shouldn't drink and drive. In other words, the message tells the listener or reader to do something good, or healthy, or charitable, rather than to buy a product.

LYRICS

If there's any one form of writing you're most familiar with, chances are it's song lyrics. You hear them every day, you probably know a ton of them by heart, but have you ever thought of writing them yourself?

Why not try?! Write a set of lyrics. But before you do, listen to a few songs with a "different ear." That is, don't listen just as a person who enjoys music. Listen to hear the structure of the lyrics, the rhyme scheme, the repetition of words, and the way the song is constructed overall.

A common question is, which comes first, the music or the lyrics? Professional songwriters work both ways; sometimes they write the music first, and sometimes the lyrics. You can try it either way. You can write a set of lyrics by itself, or you can write them to fit existing music.

FAMILY OR NEIGHBORHOOD NEWSLETTER

Hey, did you hear about Sean's new bike? How about Kate's dog winning a red ribbon in the local dog show? The Andersons' house got robbed—but the police caught the burglar. And Brad is going to spend the summer with his uncle in Minnesota.

It's all material for the neighborhood newsletter. And you can be the whole staff of the newsletter—the only reporter, the editor, the proofreader, the printer, and the distributor. But writing it is the most fun part—and the most important.

Using your best reportorial style, write up the neighborhood news that would be of interest to your friends and the other kids in the neighborhood.

As an alternative, you can create a family newsletter. Report on news from all the branches of your extended family, not only your immediate family but grandparents, cousins, and other family members. Call up as many relatives as is practical, and find out what's been happening with them.

If your family is spread across the country, consider sending out a brief email to each of the other households in your extended family, asking for all the news from their family members.

Prompt their memories by suggesting certain areas in which they might have news: Recent birthday celebrations or other happy occasions, new pets, new cars or bikes, new jobs for any of the adult family members or after-school jobs for the kids, good report cards, kids' extracurricular activities (such as band or Scouts), any sports activities the kids have been involved in (whether through the school, some other group, or just informal neighborhood games), religious celebrations or activities, any charitable or community work that family members might have been involved in (such as helping with with a food drive), news relating to their hobbies, recent trips, or plans for upcoming vacations.

In interviewing family members or neighborhood residents for newsletter articles, remember the five Ws: Who, What, When, Where, and Why. Get the basics, then get further information. Afte the interviews, when writing your articles, remember that the five Ws need to appear at or near the beginning of each.

"Cousin Nancy celebrated her tenth birthday on March 22nd with a party at the local bowling alley for ten friends" may not be brilliant creative writing, but it is a solid journalistic lead. You may choose to lead instead with "Bright yellow streamers decorated the first four lanes of the Elm City Bowling Alley on March 22nd, while eleven ten-year-olds groaned with dismay at too-frequent gutter balls." But follow up quickly with the essential facts. Your next sentnece might read, "The occasion was Cousin Nancy's tenth birthday party, celebrated by ten friends who joined her for a bowling birthday party." Don't bury the five Ws too far down in the article.

In addition to actual news, your newsletter might contain such features as an advice column, a word puzzle, or an events listing. It can also offer an interview with a particularly interesting member of the family or resident of the neighborhood. Do you have a family member who emigrated from another country? Why not interview him or her about what life was like in "the old country"? If you're doing a neighborhood newsletter, is there someone in the neighborhood—kid or adult—who has an unusual hobby or collection, lives in a house that's supposedly haunted, or has some other interesting story to tell? Interview that person.

When you've finished writing all the articles (and features, if any), you need to edit your newsletter. Editing your own work is difficult, but put it aside for a little bit, and work on a different project. Then go back to it. It won't seem quite as familiar, now, so when you read it over, you'll see it with "new eyes." Try to be critical of every aspect of your writing, from sentence structure to word choice to whether you've gotten the facts across correctly and understandably. And, naturally, be sure your grammar, spelling, and punctuation are correct.

A two-column format is better, but if you don't know how to create two columns on your computer, let each story spread clear across the page from margin to margin. You can print out multiple copies right from the computer.

WORD PUZZLES AND GAMES

There are many kinds of word puzzles and games. Probably the best known is crossword puzzles, but they are far from the only kind of word game. Cryptograms encode a word, sentence, or paragraph in a substitution code. For example, the simplest substitution code is to print a B for an A, a C for a B, a D for a C, and so on. So the word MUSIC would be written as NVTJD.

Usually codes are more complex. The next step beyond substituting B for A, C for B, and so on is to substitute a letter much farther away in the alphabet. For example, for an A substitute a J, for B write K, for C write L, for D write M, and so on.

Even better is to use a random code. In a random code, the letters that substitute for the original letters don't follow in any order. B might stand in for A, but C wouldn't substitute for B. Perhaps J is the code for B, and V is the code for C. Here's how you set it up:

Write the letters from A to Z in a row across a sheet of paper. Now write them all again, below the first row of letters, in random order. That is, write an A below any of the letters, write a B below any of the letters, then a C below any letter, and so on, but don't write them in order. When you've written all 26 letters, you've got your key.

Now think of a clever, funny, or otherwise interesting sentence (or paragraph) and encode it according to your key. If the first word is BE, look under the B and see what letter corresponds to it. Write that letter down. Now look under the E, see what the code is for E, and write that letter down. Skip a space, and encode the second word. Continue till the whole sentence or phrase is encoded.

Though encoding isn't writing, it is working with words and can be very enjoyable. The sentences or paragraphs you encode, however, can be the products of your creativity and imagination. Use your best writing talents to think of true or funny sayings you can encode.

Then there are scrambled word games. In these, you take a word, such as LIGHT and scramble the letters, perhaps coming up with TIGLH or HGTLI. The challenge to the puzzle-solver is to re-scramble the letters till he comes up with the correct word.

Be careful, in offering a scrambled word, that there aren't two possible correct answers. For instance, you might scramble the word STUDY into TUYDS, but don't offer STUDY as "the correct answer," as it is not the only correct answer. Those same letters will also re-scramble into DUSTY. Similarly, STOBA can de-scramble into either BOATS or BOAST.

Since constructing word games is a very specialized form of writing, I won't go into the various other kinds of games here. But if word games intrigue you, you can buy magazines that feature them. From these, you can see what other kinds of word games there are and learn to construct the games yourself.

Maybe someday your crossword puzzle will be featured in the pages of the Sunday New York Times. Publications do pay modest sums for various types of word games, and there are even magazines devoted entirely to such puzzles, whether crossword, word search, or some other variety.

GREETING CARDS

It used to be that men hated the word "Greetings." That was the salutation at the opening of letters from the draft board. Letters beginning "Greetings" went on to "invite" men into the Armed Forces.

But greetings can actually be very pleasant—especially the kind we're talking about here: greeting cards.

Probably you've made simple greeting cards in the past. When you were younger, you may have drawn daisies, shining suns, hearts, or Christmas trees on the front of a folded piece of paper, then written HAPPY BIRTHDAY, MOM or MERRY CHRISTMAS, DAD, or HAPPY VALENTINE'S DAY on the card. Not exactly a Hallmark original, but perfectly suitable for a seven-year-old.

You're older now.

But homemade greeting cards can be even more appreciated at your age—if you take more care with the words you put on them. Can't draw? Cut out suitable pictures from a magazine, or collaborate with a friend who has artistic talent but isn't as good with words as you are. Let him draw the pictures while you write the words. (That's how it's often done with commercially produced cards.)

If you take a look at the words on greeting cards sold in stores, you'll see you can break them down into two kinds:

Contemporary cards are usually thin and tall in shape, have relatively few words, and are often funny. Humor isn't essential though, although some sort of "punch line" is. For example, the outside of a Mother's Day card might start by saying, "A good mother is" and then list three or four complimentary adjectives. Then it might repeat, "A good mother is....." Opening the card, the recipient reads "YOU," the only word on the inside. Set-up and punch line—no humor, but the approach is light rather than sentimental and tender.

Sentimental cards, by contrast, are usually closer to square in shape, have more words, and speak from the heart rather than the funnybone. In addition, they frequently feature rhymed verse on the inside.

The cards in the store can also be broken down into two other kinds of categories: Cards for an occasion, and cards for no occasion. The most frequent occasions are birthday, holiday, graduation, condolence, wedding, and anniversary. "No-occasion" cards may be sent to say "I love you," "I'm thinking of you," "I'm glad you're my friend," "Thank you for being there when I needed you," or "You're such a good friend, and you proved it," or even "I'm sorry for what I said/did." Some no-occasion cards don't even express one of those sentiments; they just comment on life in a humorous way.

Whether the sentiment inside is a rhymed verse, an unrhymed verse, or not verse at all, it needs to be brief and to the point, as well as thoughtful or clever or both. It needs to keep in mind both the sender of the card and the intended recipient. Who is likely to send this card? Who is he or she likely to send it to? A best friend? A parent? A boyfriend or girlfriend? A favorite teacher? A sister or brother?

Try for sincerity along with brevity, writing from

your heart, as if you were the person sending the card. What would someone buying a card want to say to her or his best friend, grandma, or whoever the card is for?

If you've never thought much about greeting cards, the different kinds there are, or how they're set up, visit a local store and examine their selection with a new pair of eyes: You're not looking at the cards as a consumer, now. You're reading them to learn how they're written, what the different kinds are, how few or many words are typically included in a card, and everything else you can learn by studying them.

Whatever you write—greeting cards, books, poems, articles, stories, or some other form of writing—studying the market is important for a professional writer. If you're writing a book, you need to know which publishers are buying that type of book before you decide where to send it. If you're writing an article for a magazine, you need to familiarize yourself with that magazine in order to know how to "tailor" the article—that is, how to write it to make it fit the format of that magazine.

Are their articles aimed at men, women or both? Older or younger? Better educated or less so? Do they want articles written in an authoritative tone of voice or a chatty one? What length? How do their articles usually begin—with facts, with an anecdote, with a question ("What would you do if you found shoplifted merchandise in your child's closet?"), with a quotation?

And if you were trying to sell greeting card verses to a company, you'd study greeting cards in general, and that company's cards in particular, to get a feel for the market. What sort of cards are currently popular? What sort of cards are mostly published by the particular company you're interested in selling to?

Study the market now, even though you're not really trying to sell your greeting card verse. It will get you more familiar with greeting cards. It will also get you used to the idea of studying your market to know what various publishers are buying.

When you have a better feel for how a greeting card is written, go home and try writing several. (Tip: Before you go to the trouble of constructing an actual card, write your ideas on paper first. Not every idea is going to be worthwhile. Not every verse will be suitable.)

You might want to first write down your ideas for greeting card sentiments, and whether these are ideas for sentimental or funny cards, for poetic greetings or greetings not in verse form. Then develop each idea—or cross it off the list if you find it's not such a good idea after all. Finally, sift through your finished verses or other sentiments and decide which ones are worth making cards out of.

Now get to work making actual cards (you can use posterboard or construction paper), using the words you've written.

Present them with pride to family aor friends, knowing you've written something more than just "I LOVE YOU, MOM." Since your cards come from the heart—and spring from your creative mind as well—your family and friends will treasure them. And you've gotten practice at another form of writing.

AESOP REVISITED

Aesop was famous for his fables, fictional stories that convey lessons to the reader. When the slow and steady tortoise beats the rapid hare through diligence and perseverance, readers can learn, from the fictional characters, a lesson that applies in real life: Slow and steady wins the race.

Fables most commonly feature animals, or sometimes inanimate objects, though a fable can depict ficitonal humans as well. A fable has a point; it's not just a story written for amusement's sake, but one that teaches a lesson or moral value.

Try writing at least one fable. (Hint: You'll probably want to first decide on the lesson the fable will deliver, before you choose your plot or characters.)

BALLOONS THAT DON'T FLOAT

Not everyone involved with the production of comics is an artist. Some comic strips or comic books are written by teams. One partner, the writer, writes the dialogue and a brief description of the action to be shown; the other partner, the artist, does the drawing. Many other comic strip artists work solo but buy gag lines from writers.

A writer dreams up one day's comic strip for an existing comic. Then she or he writes, on an index card, a brief description of the action to be depicted in the strip, along with the words to be lettered in the "balloons" (or underneath the picture, in the case of certain comics, particularly "one-panel" comics).

Of course this is applicable only to funny comic strips, not those that tell a continuing story.

Though it's unlikely that you can sell a comic strip gag to an artist at this point, you can do something similar as practice. If your drawing ability is passable, of course you can draw the strip (or single-panel comic) yourself.

But assuming it isn't, you can cut pictures out of magazines, pasting two together if need be, and dream up a funny caption or dialogue. (Cut speech balloons out of white paper and paste them down in appropriate spots on the picture.) Or white out the dialogue in an existing comic, replacing it with your own dialogue.

SPEECHES

Are you or a friend campaigning for a post such as class president or student council treasurer? If not, are you in favor of someone who's running for some kind of office, even if that person isn't a particular friend of yours?

Write a campaign speech (or victory speech) for that person. The best way to begin the speech is with an attention-getting statement or story. If you choose a story, it can be true or a joke, but either way it should in some way be relevant to the main point or opening point of the speech. After that, say what has to be said quickly, and wrap up with a memorable finish.

At appropriate points throughout the speech, humor is welcome though not essential. It does help keep the speech from getting boring, though. And it helps get the audience on the speaker's side.

After you've written the first draft of the speech, try reading it aloud, preferably with a recorder going. Play back the recording and listen to the speech with a critical ear. Does it sound like someone speaking—or like someone reading an essay? Writing words to be spoken is different from writing words to be read silently to yourself.

DIARIES AND JOURNALS

It's not just girls and women who keep diaries. Such famous men as Henry David Thoreau, Ralph Waldo Emerson, Nathaniel Hawthorne, Walt Whitman, and Samuel Pepys kept diaries as well. And then there are journals, similar to diaries but more generally acceptable to men. While diaries and journals aren't written with the intent of their being published, occasionally, as with Anne

Frank's diary, they do get printed.

However, getting a diary or journal published isn't the main point of keeping one. Whether you keep a journal/diary to remember these years in years to come, or as a means of sorting out events that happen to you, when you write in that book, you're practicing your craft.

Not, of course, if your entries read like this: "Eggs for breakfast. Sunny. Schoolbus late. Pop quiz in English. Ms. Harrold out sick, sub was a real nerd. Skipped the cafeteria lunch—mystery meat. Fought with Lee. I hate homework."

No, to make journal- or diary-keeping meaningful to you as an aspiring writer, write full and descriptive sentences that flow. Describe the world around you— the eggs, the weather, the impatience of the other kids waiting for the late schoolbus. In what way was the sub a nerd? What did the mystery meat look and smell like? Why did you fight with Lee, and who won?

Don't just write a "skeleton" account of the day. Pad out that skeleton with the flesh of description, the meat that makes reading it worthwhile. In years to come, you'll enjoy rereading your journal/diary that much more if your words recall for you the way the sunlight gleamed off the bald principal's head—or the exquisiteness of the snowflake you let melt on your finger. And, in the meanwhile, you'll be honing your skills as a writer.

By the way, you also ought to carry a pocket-sized notebook and pen with you at all times, unless you have a smartphone with a note-keeping feature. This is to write in, too, though not in the same way as a journal or diary. Some of the uses of a notebook are:

• To make notes in when you're away from home and get a great idea for a story, article, poem, etc. Jot down the bare-bones plot, or key words, or whatever will preserve the idea for you till you can get home and actually write the piece itself.

• To jot observations of things you see, hear,

smell, touch, or taste that might work their way into your writing at a later date.

• To record snippets of real-life conversations that you want to preserve for later use in your writing.

• To practice writing in when you have time to fill. Are you waiting in the dentist's waiting room, sidelined by an injury during PE class, sitting in study hall with your homework all done, or waiting on a corner for a friend who's late? Utilize the time by practicing writing believable dialogue or attention-grabbing leads. Dream up some great titles. Create some interesting characters around whom you can build a story later. Or actually start your next story.

FUNNY, BUT NOT ON YOUR REPORT CARD

Riddle: What's funny, but not on your report card?
Answer: Parodies (pair o' Ds)
It's a lame joke, but it's suited to the topic—parodies, a kind of humor. Parodies poke fun at something already existing—such as a poem or song, a magazine or book, a famous work of art—by changing the words or appearance of the item that's being parodied.

The famous picture known as "Whistler's mother" has been depicted in slightly altered form—with the woman's lips pursed, so that she appears to be whistling. That's a form of parody. If you put together a magazine—or even a mock magazine made of construction paper—called it GLAD, and showed a doltish guy similar to Mad's Alfred E. Neumann, with his features distorted in an outrageously broad grin, you'd have a parody.

And of course, of all forms of the arts, the written word lends itself to parody most easily.

Take the famous proverb: "Early to bed and early to rise/Makes a man healthy, wealthy, and wise." That's been parodied in many forms. One example is, "Early to rise and early to bed/Makes a man healthy, wealthy, and dead."

Famous parodist/satirist Stan Freberg combined the story of St. George and the Dragon with the old radio/TV police program Dragnet to come up with "St. George and the Dragonet," in which St. George, sounding much like Dragnet's officer Joe Friday, goes out looking for dragons. It was written in the style of the Dragnet program. Jack Webb, who starred in the show as Friday, had a distinctive way of speaking, and in Freberg's version, St. George's lines were spoken in the manner used by Webb as Friday.

Songs are particularly good targets for parody. Much of the late Allan Sherman's work was parodies. "Down by the Riverside" became "Don't Buy the Liverwurst," and "The Yellow Rose of Texas" became "I'm Melvin Rose from Texas."

A parody, then, uses an original piece of writing or art, changing it so that it resembles the original recognizably, yet is different in a funny way. Suppose you live in Pennsylvania, and you've recently had some really bad weather—say, two days of very high winds, followed by three days of drenching rains. You could write a parody to the tune of "Oklahoma," which might begin, "Pennsylvania/Where the wind is followed by the rain."

Write at least one parody; write several, if you can. These can be parodies of anything, though your most likely targets are songs or song titles, and proverbs.

CAPTIONS OUTRAGEOUS

How's your talent for humor writing? Not every writer is a humorist, but you never know till you try. The exercise in replacing comic strip dialogue with your own gave you an opportunity to try your hand at writing one type of humor; here's a chance to test out your abilities with another kind.

Your mission is to look through old photos and find some that have humorous possibilities, then write captions to go along with the photos. They may be photos that are intentionally humorous, such as pictures of kids with blueberry-smeared faces, or people dressed in outrageous clothes for a costume or theme party.

They may also be pictures whose humorous appearance was unintentional. Virtually everyone has taken one picture in which the subject was standing in front of a thin tree. When the picture was developed, the tree appeared to be growing out of the subject's head! Other photographic accidents with humorous potential include:

• A runner blurring his way through the picture as the shutter clicks

• Rover lifting his leg against a tree just when the photographer snaps the picture

• Someone posed unintentionally near a sign whose words are funny in contrast with the picture. (Examples: a small child in her toy car next to a sign that says NO PARKING. A man dressed as a hobo for a costume party, posed on a street within sight of a store's sign that says FINE SUITS AND COATS.)

Find in your photo collection any pictures that have possibilities for humorous captions, and caption them.

PART THREE

Write on!

Okay, you've tried your hand at a lot of different kinds of writing. In terms of stories and articles, you've learned about and practiced beginnings, endings, dialogue, and more. Now it's time to apply what you've learned and... write! I want you to write a whole story or article, from beginning to end. In fact, I want you to write four.

Yes, I said four. But don't let that scare you. You've gotten this far. All the instructions...all the homework...all the work involved haven't all scared you off. You really do want to be a writer. That's great! But now, you need to put it all together and write!

You may think you are interested only in writing stories, or you may be interested strictly in writing biographies, or essays. But you need to get practiced at various kinds of writing, not just the kind you're most interested in. You never know where life will lead you.

First of all, you might set out to have a career writing fiction. Yet it's not that easy to make a living as a freelance writer, and staff jobs writing fiction just aren't that common. One day you might be offered a job writing newspaper articles, or biographies, or science textbooks, or speeches. It's not the kind of writing you have your heart set on doing, but realistically you know you have three choices:

1 - Turn down the job, spend all your time writing novels or short stories, and worry about where the grocery money is going to come from.

2 - Turn down the job and take an office job or a sales job or some other job that's not only far from the sort of writing you want to do but is far afield from writing altogether.

3 - Take the job, knowing it's not the kind of writing you'd really like to do, but at least it's a writing job. You can still work on your novel at night and weekends (and you'll find it's a lot easier concentrating when you don't have to worry about whether you're going to have enough money to pay the rent). Too, your day job will be much more enjoyable if it's something in the writing field, even if it's not the field of writing you most enjoy.

Now...which are you going to choose? Choice number one, two, or three? Most of you will choose number three. Of course, your interest might not be fiction but writing essays—and it might even be that the day job does involve writing fiction. But you get the general point I'm trying to make.

So, now you see one reason that it's important to be a well-rounded writer, one who can write both fiction and nonfiction, and hopefully different types of nonfiction as well.

Another reason, at your age, is...your age. You're still young enough that your interests might change. Three or five or eight years from now, you might find yourself attracted to a totally different area of the writing field, one that holds no interest for you now.

So...keeping in mind everything you've learned from this book, write at least two articles or essays (nonfiction) and at least two stories (fiction).

There are no assigned topics. You're free to write on any subject you want. But just in case you're drawing a blank, wondering what the heck to write about, I do have some suggestions. You may choose from among them or write on something completely different. Here are the suggestions:

The Dinosaur (or Dragon) in the Park
The Martians Have Landed
My TV Show (not My Favorite TV Show)
The Worst Thing In the World
The Attic Holds a Secret
If I Were Invisible
After "Happily Ever After"
My Favorite Sounds (or Smells, Tastes, etc.)
I Would Not Want To Live Without _____
The Person I Admire the Most

I am not giving you a length requirement. When you write for school, you are probably told how many words or pages to turn in. If you become a staff writer on a newspaper or magazine, you will also be told to write each story or article a certain length. And even as a freelancer, if you write articles you will find that most magazines have a minimum and maximum length they will consider. (As a book writer, you'll have more freedom.)

But for this assignment, I'm not giving you a word length requirement. Just do your best, and remember everything you've learned in this book—starting with the title. Ready? Set? Write!

Like Marble, Writing Needs to Be Polished

Do you think that once you've written each of your four stories or articles, the story is finished? It isn't! You may be glad to be done with it by the time you've labored over it for a while. In the case of writing for publication, you may be eager to send your manuscript right off to a publisher when you've finished it. But wait!

Any story (article, book) needs polishing. Every story (article, book) needs editing and revising. "But that's the editor's job!" I can hear you saying. And, to a certain extent, that's true. But only partly.

Just for a minute, pretend you're an editor. You work for a magazine, newspaper, or book publisher. You have to edit many manuscripts, you don't get paid overtime for staying past 5:00, and you have deadlines—you have to get each issue of the magazine edited within a month, or get a newspaper edited in a day, or get a certain number of books edited each season.

Let's use a magazine editor as an example. You have an opening in your next issue, and you have two articles you might be interested in using in that slot. Each of them is on a topic appropriate to your magazine. Each of them is the right length. Each of them is interesting. But one is very well written, neat, with few mistakes; the other is sloppy, not as well written, and contains several spelling and grammar errors. It's going to need a lot more work, a lot more editing, to make it ready to use in the magazine.

Which one are you going to use in the issue? Which one are you going to send back to the author with a rejection slip?

There's another reason, too, that editors often reject manuscripts with careless mistakes or sloppy writing. An editor who gets an article with a misspelling such as "recieve" for "receive" is going to wonder if that's all that's wrong: Are your facts in error too? Or were you just as sloppy about looking up facts as you were about checking your spelling, your grammar, your writing?

So before you send off anything you've written, before you say, "It's finished," go over it a couple of times for errors and for ways you can improve your writing.

Check your spelling. (A computer spell-checker is helpful but not foolproof; for instance, if you typo "bought" for "brought," the spell-checker won't catch it, since "bought" is a legitimate word.)

Check your grammar. Have you avoided making any mistakes you should have known better than to make?

Check your facts. Is every "fact" you've presented verified as correct?

Check your writing. Polish it. Make it sparkle. Have you used a cliché or tired, overworked simile that might best be replaced by a less overused phrase? Does the writing seem leaden, heavy, less than sparkling anywhere in what you've written? You want your writing to be better than just "all right."

If it's fiction, does your plot make sense? Is the ending consistent with what happened during the story? Do your characters and their dialogue ring true—do they act and speak like real people, and like people in their circumstances would act and speak? You haven't "telegraphed" the ending—made what was supposed to be a surprise ending so obvious well in advance that there was no surprise at all?

Not every ending is supposed to be a surprise, of course. Sometimes we know that a character is going to die by the book's end, or that a couple is going to get married. But the scene still has to pack an emotional punch. In the majority of books and stories, however, you don't want your readers to know in advance just exactly how it's going to turn out.

If it's nonfiction, have you not only got all your facts right but presented them in an appropriate order? Have you made your writing interesting? Dull, boring prose never won over a reader—or an editor.

If it's an opinion essay, have you presented your case persuasively? If it's appropriate, have you presented

84

facts in support of your opinion? Have you helped lead the reader to the ability to see things your way, or at least understand why your view is what it is, rather than just stuffing your opinion down his or her throat?

It's best to revise your writing more than once, and to let some time go by—at least a day, in most cases—between revisions. You can do your first revision right after you finish writing the piece, or you can put it down and return to it later. But it's best to get a little distance from it—at least to let it sit overnight—before you revise it again.

Look for mistakes—in typing, spelling, facts, or details. (For instance, in fiction, does a character have blonde hair in one chapter, brown in another?) Look for poor writing—or good writing that can be made even better. Polish your writing. Then polish it some more.

Only then is it truly finished.

Now that you understand the need for polishing and editing your work, go back over the four pieces you just wrote, and make them as much improved, as close to perfect, as you can.

Ready, Aim, Fire!

Unless you're writing only for your own satisfaction, you most likely want to get your book, story, article, or essay published. Where do you start? You need to know what markets to aim for, what publishers are most likely to accept your work.

At your age, a good place to start is a local newspaper—not a big daily paper, if you live in a large metropolitan area, but a smaller paper. If your local daily paper is the New York Times or some similar major paper, perhaps try a smaller local weekly. Then there is your school newspaper. You also might belong to an organization, club, or other group that has a newspaper or newsletter that would welcome some of your writing.

And when your writing improves, and you're ready for the Big Leagues?

You need a tool of the trade—a market listings book. The granddaddy of them all, and undoubtedly the best, is Writer's Market. Issued annually in the late summer, Writer's Market lists magazines, book publishers, and other places to sell your writing. Do not ever use an out-of-date edition. Market conditions (names of editors, what editors are looking for, length requirements, and so forth) change from year to year. You need the most up-to-date information at all times. The book isn't inexpensive, but most libraries have copies, so if you can't afford to buy Writer's Market every year, the library is your best friend. (Typically the book is a "reference copy"—that is, it has to be used in the library. It may not be borrowed and taken home. So bring paper and pen, or a laptop computer or other device with which to take notes, and plan to spend some time in the library.)

There are other books, too, that list markets for your work, including several put out by the publishers of Writer's Market that address specific areas of publishing. Children's Writers and Illustrators Market is one of these.

In the case of selling to magazines, it's good to get a sample copy of any magazine you're interested in writing for. Again, you may be able to find such a copy in the library, if you don't want to buy a copy of every magazine you have a professional interest in. Some magazine publishers will send a sample copy—usually a back issue (that means not the latest one) to a writer who sends an SASE. (An SASE is a self-addressed stamped envelope—a large envelope addressed to yourself, with enough postage to pay for mailing the magazine).

Reading through the magazine will give you a better feel for what sort of stories the editors are buying. You want to know about the topics that interest them and also the style of writing. Is the magazine looking for short, factual articles that are relatively straightforward? Do they want a more chatty style of writing, more informal? Do they welcome humor in your writing?

In the case of book publishers, style of writing is less relevant. Your question with book publishers is primarily what subjects they cover. Their listing in Writer's Market (or another market book of that type) will help.

Another help is their current catalogue. Most publishers will send a free catalogue if you send an SASE with a request. (In estimating postage, you can figure that most catalogs weigh only a few ounces, except in the case of a large publisher that publishes many books each season.)

Now, what about your manuscript? What should it look like?

The cover page of your book, or the top of page 1 of your article or story, should have your name, postal address, phone number, and email address in the upper left-hand corner. In the upper right, you definitely need a word count (your computer word processing programs can count the words for you), and perhaps a one- or two-word description of what you've written: "juvenile fiction," "novel," "essay," "article," "romance novel," "religious nonfiction."

If you're sending a book to more than one publisher at a time, type "SIMULTANEOUS SUBMISSION" in the upper right-hand corner, too. (With a very few exceptions, it's not acceptable to send articles or stories to more than one publisher at a time.)

All this information is typed single-spaced.

In the middle of the page, centered, type the title. Under it type "by" and then your byline—that is, the name you want your writing published under. In most cases this will be your right name, but it may not be. You may want to use a short form of your name ("Kathy" for "Katherine") or even another name altogether. (For instance, if you write both romance novels and religious fiction, you may prefer to use different names for the two. Or if you have a name that you don't think sounds very attractive, you may prefer a pseudonym—a name other than your real name—as your byline. [But note that your true name is the name to use in the upper left-hand corner.])

If this is a book, go to the next page before you start writing. If this is an article or story, you may begin on the lower half of page 1. And now you need to double-space. The manuscript itself—after the information at the top of page 1—should always be double-spaced. Your margins should be an inch to an inch-and-a-half on each side.

Many publishers these days accept emailed submissions. Some accept only emailed submissions. But there are still some that accept submissions only by postal mail. If you're "snailmailing" your manuscript, don't forget to enclose an SASE. In this case, it should be large enough for the manuscript, with the same amount of postage as you need for the outgoing envelope.

Keep track of where you're sending your manuscripts. Keep a file for each piece of writing you send out. List the date you sent it, the publisher you sent it to (including address), and the name of the editor to whose attention you sent it. (If you can get an editor's name from the listing in whichever market book you refer to, use that editor's name.)

Do not call after a week to say, "Did you get my story? Did you like it?" Always wait three months before sending a letter of inquiry. Then, if you haven't heard back from the editor, you have the right to write to her or him and, in a brief letter, state the date on which you sent the manuscript, its title, the fact that you enclosed the requisite SASE, and the fact that three months have gone by without your having heard back from the editor, which is why you're now inquiring about your manuscript.

The End of This Book Is Just the Beginning

OK—you've finished this book, but you're not finished with it. To begin with, few of us can read, absorb, and remember a whole book's worth of information in one reading. Second, now that you've read the whole book, you can do some of the earlier assignments over again and do them better.

No, I am not asking you to do all the homework all over again. But you have gained some knowledge with each new section of the book, and hopefully you can do most of the assignments in the book better than you could have the first time you did them. So I want you to do two things:

First, go back over all the assignments you did and revise them. All writers need to revise their work—not just beginners. Look over the material you wrote as you read this book, and see what improvements you can make in what you wrote. You know more now. And, a couple of chapters ago, you specifically learned about making revisions, polishing your work, and checking for errors. Use what you've learned throughout the book to improve the writing you did as you read the book.

Second, look over all the homework the book gives. Select some of it to tackle all over again. You might choose just those assignments you feel you could do much better at now. You might choose only those assignments that interest you, or those that directly bear on the field of writing you hope to get into eventually. Whatever system you choose is fine, but do some of the homework again.

Does it seem like there's a lot to remember about writing? Lots more rules and ways to do things than you ever realized there are? Relax. It will all come to you naturally, without thinking, in just a little while. But you need to practice. The more you write, the more easily it will all come to you.

Soon you'll be writing more effortlessly than ever—and you'll be using everything you've learned in this book, and writing better. Enjoy yourself. Writing is fun! Class dismissed.